'Ilse Oosterlaken has been at the forefront of developing insights on the role and importance of technology in the capability approach. *Technology and Human Development* is a major contribution to the literature on the capability approach, and it also illuminates the importance of the capability approach for anyone working on technology.'

Ingrid Robeyns, Utrecht University, the Netherlands

'Engineers are commonly committed by their professional codes of ethics to holding paramount public safety, health and welfare in their design, construction, operation and management of a progressively engineered world. The standard engineering education curriculum, however, involves little learning about public welfare. Ilse Oosterlaken's good book on *Technology and Human Development*, by engaging with the capability approach to welfare economics pioneered by Nobel Prize economist Amartya Sen, is a valuable contribution to enhancing the welfare regarding capabilities of engineering and engineers.'

Carl Mitcham, Colorado School of Mines, USA

'With a remarkable interdisciplinary approach, philosopher and engineer Ilse Oosterlaken discusses how technologies could contribute to expanding the capabilities and agency of people. In a very intelligent manner, she studies the technology–capability relationship in two ways: a "zooming in" on the design details and "zooming out" to the embedding of technical artefacts in society. The result is a compelling book essential for those interested in approaching technology from a social justice perspective.'

Alejandra Boni, Universitat Politècnica de València, Spain

'Technologies have a key role to play in human development as envisioned by the radically pluralist capability approach. This insightful book is a milestone contribution in this rapidly expanding area of enquiry, skilfully connecting the conceptual spaces of the capability approach with design studies, science and technology studies and philosophy of technology. Based on carefully chosen case studies, Ilse Oosterlaken convincingly explains how the analysis needs to include both an examination of the design details and an account of the socio-technical networks in which they are embedded. Significantly, she points out that the capabilities approach is a useful lens to examine technology use not just in the global South, but globally.'

Dorothea Kleine, University of London, UK, and author of Technolog

'For years, Ilse Oosterlaken has been doing cutting-edge research that brings together two important strands of theory that typically are only addressed by separate communities: philosophy of technology and the capabilities approach. *Technology and Human Development* captures her central insights and presents the most mature articulation of them to date. It is essential reading for both academics and practitioners interested in the topic.'

Evan Selinger, Rochester Institute of Technology, USA

TECHNOLOGY AND HUMAN DEVELOPMENT

This book introduces the capability approach – in which well-being, agency and justice are the core values – as a powerful normative lens to examine technology and its role in development. This approach attaches central moral importance to individual human capabilities, understood as effective opportunities people have to lead the kind of lives they have reason to value. The book examines the strengths, limitations and versatility of the capability approach when applied to technology, and shows the need to supplement it with other approaches in order to deal with the challenges that technology raises.

The first chapter places the capability approach within the context of broader debates about technology and human development – discussing among others the appropriate technology movement. The middle part then draws on philosophy and ethics of technology in order to deepen our understanding of the relation between technical artefacts and human capabilities, arguing that we must simultaneously 'zoom in' on the details of technological design and 'zoom out' to see the broader socio-technical embedding of a technology. The book examines whether technology is merely a neutral instrument that expands what people can do and be in life, or whether technology transfers may also impose certain views of what it means to lead a good life. The final chapter examines the capability approach in relation to contemporary debates about ICT for Development (ICT4D), as the technology domain where the approach has been most extensively applied.

This book is an invaluable read for students of development studies and science and technology studies (STS), as well as policy makers, practitioners and engineers looking for an accessible overview of technology and development from the perspective of the capability approach.

Ilse Oosterlaken is a post-doctoral researcher in the Department of Philosophy at the VU University Amsterdam, the Netherlands.

The Routledge Human Development and Capability Debates series

Series editors: Séverine Deneulin, Ortrud Leßmann and Krushil Watene

This series aims to foster multidisciplinary discussions of contemporary issues, using the normative framework of the 'capability approach' and human development paradigm. It considers the extent to which the capability approach, and its perspective of human freedom, provides useful and innovative ways of interpreting and analysing various social realities, such as well-being and justice; land conflict; indigenous rights; and technological innovation.

By highlighting both the strengths and limitations of this freedom perspective, each volume provides a comprehensive, concise and jargon-free overview of a range of contemporary challenges for postgraduate students, policy makers and practitioners.

Informed by original empirical and analytical insights, the books in this series explore innovative solutions for real-world change to foster debate in the scholarly and professional communities.

We invite book proposals which engage with a variety of fields as they relate to this ethical perspective, with a preference for those which focus on key issues or topical areas of international relevance.

Wellbeing, Justice and Development Ethics
Séverine Deneulin

Technology and Human Development
Ilse Oosterlaken

TECHNOLOGY AND HUMAN DEVELOPMENT

Ilse Oosterlaken

First published 2015
by Routledge
2 Park Square, Milton Park, Abingdon, Oxon OX14 4RN

and by Routledge
711 Third Avenue, New York, NY 10017

Routledge is an imprint of the Taylor & Francis Group, an informa business

© 2015 Ilse Oosterlaken

The right of Ilse Oosterlaken to be identified as author of this work has been asserted by her in accordance with sections 77 and 78 of the Copyright, Designs and Patents Act 1988.

All rights reserved. No part of this book may be reprinted or reproduced or utilised in any form or by any electronic, mechanical, or other means, now known or hereafter invented, including photocopying and recording, or in any information storage or retrieval system, without permission in writing from the publishers.

Trademark notice: Product or corporate names may be trademarks or registered trademarks, and are used only for identification and explanation without intent to infringe.

British Library Cataloguing-in-Publication Data
A catalogue record for this book is available from the British Library

Library of Congress Cataloging-in-Publication Data
Oosterlaken, Ilse.
Technology and human development / Ilse Oosterlaken.
pages cm
Includes bibliographical references.
1. Technology--Social aspects. 2. Economic development. 3. Technology and civilization. I. Title.
T14.5.O55 2015
303.48'3--dc23
2014044701

ISBN: 978-1-138-78057-6 (hbk)
ISBN: 978-1-138-78058-3 (pbk)
ISBN: 978-1-315-77060-4 (ebk)

Typeset in Bembo
by Fish Books Ltd.

Printed and bound in Great Britain by
TJ International Ltd, Padstow, Cornwall

CONTENTS

Acknowledgements   ix
List of figures   xi

   Introduction   1
   Of bicycles, capabilities and development   1
   Core concepts and ideas in the capability approach   3
   Capabilities and technology   7
   The capability approach as a lens to technology   9
   Aims and structure of this book   12
   References   17

1   The appropriate technology movement and the capability approach   19
   Technology as a universal fix, economic driver, or … ?   19
   The appropriate technology movement   23
   Beyond appropriate technology: agency   29
   Appropriate for whom? Gender and technology   31
   Will the real capability approach stand up?   34
   Complementary views on technology and human development   39
   References   42

viii Contents

2 The details of technological design 46
   Technical artefacts, capabilities and the good life 46
   Well-being and design 53
   The epistemological and aggregation challenge 58
   Agency and design 64
   Looking ahead: practical implementation 70
   References 73

3 Embedding technology in socio-technical networks 78
   The social nature of individual human capabilities 78
   Inserting technical artefacts in the picture 81
   Exploring some implications 84
   The system character of technology and individual freedom 90
   *Multiple realizability of capabilities and the capability–
      functioning distinction* 94
   References 101

4 A capability approach of ICT for Development (ICT4D) 103
   Is there something special about ICT? 103
   Criticisms of capability scholars on 'mainstream' ICT4D 107
   A case: mp3 players in Zimbabwe 113
   Agency versus well-being as goals for ICT4D projects 119
   The versatility of the capability approach 126
   References 133

5 Conclusion 137

Index *145*

ACKNOWLEDGEMENTS

This book is closely tied to my doctoral research, which I undertook while working for the philosophy section of Delft University of Technology (TU Delft). To a large degree I therefore need to acknowledge the same people again that I thanked in my dissertation, and in the articles/book chapters included in that dissertation. This includes many of my colleagues in Delft.

One person deserves special mention here, and that is Sabine Roeser – my former doctoral supervisor. She set aside a part of her Aspasia grant, which she received from the Netherlands Organization for Scientific Research (NWO), to support talented female researchers for a short time after getting their doctoral degree. The invaluable extra research time that this has given me at TU Delft has enabled me to write the bulk of this book, as well as to undertake some other scholarly activities.

Over the years I have benefited from discussions with so many people, it would be impossible to acknowledge them all here. These people include Alejandra Boni, Maarten Franssen, Álvaro Fernández-Baldor, Séverine Deneulin, Neelke Doorn, Alex Frediani, David Grimshaw, Saskia Harmsen, Jeroen van den Hoven, Pim Janssen, Justine Johnstone, Prabhu Kandachar, Pramod Khadilkar, Dorothea Kleine, Sjaak Koot, Paul Lapperre, Monto Mani, Annemarie Mink, Colleen Murphy, Sammia Podeva, Ibo van de Poel, Ingrid Robeyns, Sabine Roeser, Evan Selinger, Lalaine Siruno, Yingqin Zheng and Rafael Ziegler. Apologies to those I have not included here who deserve it.

A special mention should also be extended to Séverine Deneulin, Neelke Doorn, Martin van Hees, Dorothea Kleine, Niels Lammers, Annemarie Mink and Ingrid Robeyns for reviewing either the full manuscript or one or more chapters. Their comments and suggestions have been most helpful in making improvements, and of course the usual disclaimer applies that its remaining weaknesses are entirely mine.

Finally, I would like to thank co-authors and publishers for granting permission to reuse parts of previously published material in this book:

- Oosterlaken, I. (2009). Design for Development: A Capability Approach. *Design Issues* 25(4):91–102 (in Chapter 2).
- Oosterlaken, I. (2011). Inserting Technology in the Relational Ontology of Sen's Capability Approach. *Journal of Human Development and Capabilities* 12(3):425–32 (in Chapter 3).
- Oosterlaken, I., Grimshaw, D.J. and Janssen, P. (2012). Marrying the Capability Approach, Appropriate Technology and STS: The Case of Podcasting Devices in Zimbabwe. In: Oosterlaken, I. and Van den Hoven, J. (eds), *The Capability Approach, Technology and Design*. Dordrecht: Springer, pp. 113–33 (in Chapter 4).
- Oosterlaken, I. (2012). The Capability Approach and Technology: Taking Stock and Looking Ahead. In Oosterlaken, I., and Van den Hoven, J. (eds), *The Capability Approach, Technology and Design*. Dordrecht: Springer, pp. 3–26 (in Chapter 1).
- Oosterlaken, I. (2014). Human Capabilities in Design for Values. In: Van den Hoven, J., Van de Poel, I. and Vermaas, P.E. (eds), *Handbook of Ethics, Values and Technological Design*. Dordrecht: Springer (in Chapter 2).

FIGURES

0.1	Different types of capabilities as research focus points	10
0.2	The technology–capability relationship: 'zooming in' and 'zooming out'	15
2.1	The basic triangle 'technical artefacts–human capabilities–the good life'	48
2.2	Adding social practices to the basic triangle	51
2.3	Extending the triangle with persuasive or behaviour-steering technology	68
3.1	The system/network view of technology further complicating the triangle	92
4.1	The 'zooming in–zooming out' movement applied to the case	114
4.2	Network surrounding mp3 players in April–July 2010 (source: Janssen 2010)	117
4.3	Discussed technological alternatives on Kleine's (2011) determinism continuum	125
4.4	The choice framework developed by Kleine (2013)	129

INTRODUCTION

Of bicycles, capabilities and development

Do Bicycles Equal Development in Mozambique? was the somewhat odd title of a book that appeared some years ago (Hanlon and Smart 2008). Bicycles? What would make one ask a question like that? In their introductory chapter the authors describe the case of Felito Julião. That a person like him has a bicycle, the authors note, was uncommon in Mozambique a decade before. Julião uses the bicycle to earn a living, by transporting and selling sugar cane. In this way he earns 1.5 times as much as he would have earned without the bicycle. If he had to walk, he would only be able to transport one bundle of cane at a time, or perhaps in that situation he would not sell sugar cane but work on a neighbour's field instead. The authors of the book then go on to explain why they asked the question about equating bicycles with development. This question (p. 2):

> reflects the response we received when we told people we were writing a book about Mozambican development. Everyone responded in the same way: there are more bicycles. That is true. We saw bicycles everywhere and each chapter of this book is headed by a photo of someone using a bicycle, often to carry other people or large loads. *But are bicycles an accurate measure of development?* There are more cars, as well. But most people still walk. Houses are another measure of

development. In Maputo, there is a surprising number of houses costing hundreds of thousands of dollars, and it looks as if there is development. Driving through rural Nampula province, we certainly saw many villages with one or two improved houses, built of blocks or bricks and with metal sheets or tile roofs. But most people live in mud or wattle and daub houses with thatched roofs. Bouncing along the terrible road from Nampula to Ribáuè, we saw much less development. [emphasis added]

The rest of their book investigates whether there is indeed development in Mozambique. Two things in the above quote are of particular interest for the purposes of this book. The first is that the authors note that, measured in terms of car access and home ownership, a lot of inequality still exists in Mozambique. The second is their question whether bicycles are an accurate indicator of development.

The question of how to best assess or measure development and inequality has been given an interesting and influential answer in the oeuvre of Amartya Sen (1979, 1985, 1999), who won the 1998 Nobel Prize for his work in welfare economics. His work on the capability approach has among others provided part of the intellectual foundations for the human development paradigm of the United Nations Development Program (UNDP). Another major scholarly source for the capability approach is the work of philosopher Martha Nussbaum (2000, 2011).[1] These two thinkers both argue that assessment of development progress should not be made in terms of income or resource possession, but in terms of valuable individual human capabilities – or what people are effectively able to do and be. Examples are the capabilities to be healthy and to have meaningful social relations. The capability approach conceptualizes development as a process of expanding such valuable capabilities for each and every person, so that they have the real and effective freedom to realize a life they have reason to value.[2] According to a recent introduction this approach[3]

> is generally understood as a conceptual framework for a range of normative exercises, including most prominent the following: (1) the assessment of individual well-being; (2) the evaluation and assessment of social arrangements; and (3) the design of policies and proposals about social change in society.
>
> *(Robeyns 2011: §1)*

In the past decades, people have started to apply the capability approach to a range of areas and issues, including health, education, disability and gender (Robeyns 2006). This book explores how the capability approach can be brought to bear on technology. Mirroring the three exercises mentioned by Robeyns in the quote above, this book discusses the evaluation and assessment of technology (exercise 2), and the design of technical artefacts and the development of socio-technical networks as ways to bring about a positive social change (exercise 3). The term 'evaluate' already indicates that defining the values against which to make judgements is inherently part of such exercises. The core claim of the capability approach is that people's 'freedom to achieve well-being is of primary moral importance' (Robeyns 2011: 1). This is the value that should – according to capability scholars – be central in our evaluative exercises. In the capability approach 'freedom to achieve well-being' is further conceptualized in terms of *valuable* individual capabilities. The capability approach as a conceptual framework can be applied in a purely descriptive way, for example when a study merely makes an inventory of which capabilities people have or explains to which capabilities some social arrangement or technology contributes. However, often the capability approach is used in a normative way, to make a judgement about whether people's lives are going *well* or whether some social arrangement or technology is *good* to have. For this reason, in the quote above Robeyns describes the capability approach as 'a conceptual framework for a range of *normative* exercises' (emphasis added).

Core concepts and ideas in the capability approach

The bicycle, in all its simplicity, makes for a good example to further introduce some core concepts and ideas of the capability approach. Further elaborating on the example of the bicycle also provides a first rough sketch of the complex and multifaceted relation between technology and human capabilities – which will be further discussed in the chapters to come. As it happens, the bicycle has been used in the early literature on the capability approach to explain its rationale:

> Having a bike gives a person the ability to move about in a certain way that he may not be able to do without the bike. So the transportation characteristic of the bike gives the person the capability of moving in a certain way. That capability may give the person utility or happiness if he seeks such movement or finds it pleasurable. So there is, as it were,

> a sequence from a commodity (in this case a bike), to characteristics (in this case, transportation), to capability to function (in this case, the ability to move), to utility (in this case, pleasure from moving).
>
> It can be argued that it is the third category – that of capability to function – that comes closest to the notion of standard of living. The commodity ownership or availability itself is not the right focus since it does not tell us what the person can, in fact, do. I may not be able to use the bike if – say – I happen to be handicapped. Having the bike – or something else with that characteristic – may provide the basis for a contribution to the standard of living, but it is not in itself a constituent part of that standard.
>
> *(Sen 1983: 160)*

A technical term often used in the capability approach is that of 'conversion factors' that play a positive or negative role in the 'translation' from a resource into a capability. The term refers to any factor that needs to be 'right' as a precondition for expanding a person's capability by means of a resource. In the example above, a personal conversion factor – being disabled – blocks the expansion of the capability of moving around. One could also think of other factors, not mentioned by Sen, obstructing or facilitating the expansion of human capabilities by means of bicycles. A person in the Netherlands – a country which has good roads and even many separate bicycle lanes – will gain more capabilities from owning a bicycle than a Bedouin living in the desert. This is an example of environmental conversion factors. And ownership of a bicycle hardly expands the capabilities of women in Saudi Arabia, as local religious authorities unfortunately do not allow them to cycle[4] – thus a cultural or social conversion factor is problematic in this example. The example of bicycles and women in Saudi Arabia may also serve to illustrate why – according to Sen – capabilities are not only a better indicator of quality of life than resources, but also a better indicator than subjective well-being (such as happiness, desire satisfaction or utility, 'in this case, pleasure from moving'). Sen (1983: 160) says the following about this:

> while utility reflects the use of the bike, it does not concentrate on the use itself, but on the mental reaction to that use. If I am of a cheerful disposition and enjoy life even without being able to move around, because I succeed in having my heart leap up every time I behold a rainbow in the sky, I am no doubt a happy person, but it does not follow that I have a high standard of living ... So the constituent part

of the standard of living is not the good, nor its characteristics, but the ability to do various things by using that good or those characteristics, and it is that ability rather than the mental reaction to that ability in the form of happiness that, in this view, reflects the standard of living.

We can imagine that some women in Saudi Arabia might adjust their preferences under the influence of the society in which they grow up, and no longer wish to go places by bicycle (or other means of transportation). Extreme poverty may, Sen fears, sometimes have the same effect on people's aspirations and expectations. This is what he calls the problem of adaptive preferences. It is one of the reasons why he proposes to focus on capabilities when assessing inequality and development. Because people in poor areas in the world may have adjusted their expectations and aspirations, they may experience equal levels of happiness or satisfaction with (aspects of) their life as people living in wealthy areas. According to the capability approach we can however not simply conclude from this that there is no moral need for initiatives to reduce poverty. At the same time we should be careful not to label people's preferences too easily as 'adaptive'. A careful ethical evaluation of preferences is needed before doing so. The reason is that the capability approach acknowledges that people may hold very different yet legitimate ideas about what a good life consists of and that people should be able to make their own life choices accordingly. In other words: the capability approach has a high regard for human agency. 'Agency' refers to the ability that humans have to reflect on what they value, to set goals and to pursue the realization of those goals. 'The opposite of a person with agency', Alkire (2005a: 3) argues, 'is someone who is forced, oppressed, or passive'. Crocker and Robeyns (2010) distinguish four dimensions in Sen's understanding of agency: self-determination, reason orientation and deliberation, action, and impact on the world. Without having sufficient capabilities, people would not be able to take certain actions and/or make an impact on the world.

Respect for human agency is the main reason why the capability approach makes a theoretical distinction between 'capabilities' and 'functionings'. This is a distinction, so Robeyns (2005: 95) explains, 'between the realized [functionings] and the effectively possible [capabilities]; in other words, between achievements on the one hand, and freedoms or valuable options from which one can choose on the other'. From a normative perspective it may make a difference whether one focuses on the functionings or the capabilities of people. An example that capability scholars regularly refer to (e.g. Alkire 2005a) is that a person who is fasting may reach a condition that seems similar to a person who is starving. Both are undernourished and their bodily functioning is thus the same. Yet from a normative perspective there is an important difference: one person has the capability to eat but chooses not to; the other person does not have the capability. The capability approach acknowledges that people pursue not only their own well-being, but may also choose to pursue other ends. Examples are promoting the well-being of others or living up to religious ideals. The person who is fasting exercises his agency in order to achieve some goal, even though this may be at the expense of personal well-being. We need to acknowledge that people may have very different ideas of what constitutes a good life, and different preferences. According to the capability approach policy makers should therefore ideally aim at merely expanding people's capabilities and not force people into certain functionings, like being well fed. However, capability scholars recognize that there are contexts in which it is appropriate to focus on functionings (Robeyns 2011). If people have a wide-ranging set of capabilities, they are empowered to realize the kind of life they value. The implication is that 'in real life two people with identical capability sets are likely to end up with different types and levels of achieved functionings, as they make different choices following their different ideas of the good life' (Robeyns 2005: 101).

There is a further way in which agency is discussed in the capability approach literature. In his many publications Sen has repeatedly emphasized that we should not see the income-poor as passive 'patients' to be helped. Individuals and groups, according to Sen, should be enabled to be 'active participant(s) in change, rather than … passive and docile recipient(s) of instruction or of dispensed assistance' (1999: 281). For Sen, agency is not only something that is enlarged as a result of a development process, by expanding people's capability set. In Sen's view, people do not only exercise their agency in making choices in their own, personal lives. Agency should be exercised during development itself – which is not only about the outcome, but also about how we get there. People exercise their agency while bringing about change in their community and society at large – possibly contributing to goals beyond their individual well-being. Capabilities have a double role here, in the sense that they are both ends in themselves (or at least, some capabilities are) and a means for people to take charge of the development process. By exercising their agency people bring about further change in both their lives and in their community/society.

It is important to realize that the capability approach takes an interest in those human capabilities that are *intrinsically valuable*. A person may choose to turn these capabilities into functionings, which 'together constitute what makes a life valuable' to that person (Robeyns 2005: 95), they are 'constitutive of a person's being' (Alkire 2005b: 118). Examples of such intrinsically valuable capabilities are the capability to be healthy and the capability to maintain nourishing personal relations. Not all capabilities that a person may have belong to this category of intrinsically valuable capabilities. Some capabilities may be trivial from the perspective of justice and development. Having a tenth brand of washing powder available certainly adds something to the choices a person has. However Sen (1987) agrees with critics[5] that it does not expand the capabilities we have reason to value, it does not give us extra freedom to realize something of value in our life. Other capabilities may be even outright undesirable to promote. Nussbaum (2000) gives the example of the capability for cruelty – which new torture devices could certainly expand. In short: a normative evaluation of capabilities is needed. Nussbaum has for example identified a list of ten central human capabilities that are – according to her – needed for living a flourishing human life, in conformity with human dignity. She claims that justice requires bringing each and every human being over a certain threshold for each of the capabilities on her list. Although Sen gives plenty of examples of valuable capabilities in his work, he has always refused to make such a list. His reasons are that the proper list of capabilities may depend on purpose and context, and should be a result of public reasoning; not something a theorist should come up with (Robeyns 2005). Which capabilities matter, for example for evaluating development projects, is an important topic of discussion in the capability approach literature. It also raises the questions how we should decide about this and who should be involved in the decision process (Crocker 2008). These are questions which have been extensively addressed in the capability approach literature.

Capabilities and technology

Not all capabilities expanded by technologies belong to the category of intrinsically valuable capabilities. Many 'technology-enabled' capabilities have merely instrumental value, because of their contribution to intrinsically valuable capabilities. For example, a hammer and nails may expand one's capability to join timber, which may in turn be important for expanding one's capability to have adequate shelter. This capability in turn contributes to one's capability to be healthy – which is intrinsically valuable. Furthermore, some capabilities have both instrumental value and intrinsic value, in other words they are both means and ends at the same time. The bicycle example may again be used to illustrate. Generally, the freedom to go to places to which one wants to go, which is expanded by the bicycle, seems intrinsically valuable. More specifically, a mountain biker could also appreciate his capability to cycle because of the challenging outdoor experience and shared social activity it offers. For many others the capability to get about with a bicycle may be merely of instrumental value, as – for example – it may contribute to one's capability to visit friends, or to one's capability to exercise and in that way maintain good health. Having a bicycle may furthermore contribute to one's livelihood opportunities (as in the case of Felito Julião in Mozambique), which could in turn again contribute in diverse ways to other valuable capabilities. Bicycles can also be an effective means to improve access to education. Bicycles have had this effect in the Indian state of Bihar, where a project successfully made bicycles available to girls, which they could use to travel to school. Prior to the provision of bicycles many girls did not enrol in secondary school because their families could not afford public transport (Muralidharan and Prakash 2013). Gaining the capability to be educated is in turn crucial to expanding a range of other capabilities.

The previous examples all discussed the direct or indirect expansion of capabilities of people who could personally use a bicycle. However, rather than expanding the capabilities of their users, new technologies may also contribute to the capabilities of a wider group of people by changing existing social practices, or making new ones possible. There exists a Dutch development organization that runs Bike4Care projects, in which – among others – health workers visit people at home for health checks and counselling, using the bicycle as a means of transport.[6] Bicycles have also been remodelled to serve as ambulances. Such new or improved health care practices have the potential to expand the capability to remain healthy to a large group of people. The effect of technology on human capabilities may be even more indirect, through its (long-term) impact on a society's culture. According to Muralidharan and Prakash (2013), for example, the bicycle project not only led to increasing female school enrolment, but also to more safety for the girls in question as a result from cycling to school in groups. It also led to 'changes in patriarchal social norms that proscribed female mobility outside the village, which [also] inhibited female secondary school participation'. Several sources document that bicycles have in the past also played a significant role in the emancipation and empowerment of women in the global North.[7]

However, we should acknowledge that technological development projects may fail (Chapter 1 will develop this) and as a consequence not expand any instrumentally or intrinsically valuable capabilities. They may also have unintended and unexpected positive or negative effects on people's capabilities. Furthermore, the capability impacts of technologies may be mixed – they could expand one capability while at the same time reducing another, or just expand the capabilities of some group of people while reducing the capabilities of another group of people. In the latter case the introduction of the technology may raise an issue of distributive justice. Justice is, together with well-being and agency, one of the three values most extensively addressed in the capability approach literature.

One thing which may be good to make explicit at this point is that the way in which the term 'human capabilities' is used in the capability approach differs from the way in which this term – or similar terms – are used in other contexts. For example, 'human capital' is a term commonly used in innovation economics. It concerns the ability of individuals to be productive as labourers and contribute to economic value creation. The capability approach is interested in a wider range of abilities or capacities. It only takes an interest in human capital to the degree that it directly or indirectly improves people's life – and not just makes firms better off. Another common concern in innovation economics is the 'innovation capabilities' of firms or entire economic sectors. And development organizations are often working on 'capacity building' with local partner organizations, to increase the capability of these organizations to attract funding, manage development projects and so on. In both these cases the term refers to capabilities at a collective level. From the perspective of the capability approach one would ask whether increasing such collective capabilities or capacities contributes – either directly or indirectly – to expanding the capabilities of individuals to lead a flourishing human life. If they do, they have instrumental value for the ultimate end of improving people's lives. Figure 0.1 shows the distinctions made here. Whether collective capabilities can have intrinsic value is a topic of disagreement among capability scholars.

The capability approach as a lens to technology[8]

Technology has implications for well-being, agency and justice – three central values in the capability approach literature. The proposal made in this book is that the capability approach provides a powerful conceptual framework to assess and evaluate technology in terms of these values, which can

	Intrinsically valuable	**Instrumentally valuable**
Individual capabilities	Capability approach ←	Innovation economics
Collective capabilities	?	Innovation economics

Figure 0.1 Different types of capabilities as research focus points

partly be understood in terms of valuable individual capabilities. Technology is of course a complex phenomenon and there is no agreement on its essence or nature. Throughout history and in different disciplines 'technology' has been defined and understood in a range of ways, for example as a product, a process or a form of knowledge (Mitcham and Schatzberg 2009). This book is not the place to discuss this in detail. Broadly speaking, the view of technology adopted is that it concerns a set of material artefacts, or systems consisting of such artefacts, designed to perform certain functions. Intuitively, there seems to be a close link between the nature of technical artefacts and what people are able to do and be, in other words: their capabilities. It is therefore somewhat surprising that until about a decade ago the capability approach had hardly been applied to technology. Sometimes technology is even completely overlooked, as in this theoretical overview article, which gives a detailed enumeration of capability inputs:

> For some of these capabilities, the main input will be financial resources and economic production, but for others it can also be political practices and institutions, such as the effective guaranteeing and protection of freedom of thought, political participation, social or cultural practices, social structures, social institutions, public goods, social norms, traditions and habits. The capability approach thus covers all dimensions of human well-being.
> *(Robeyns 2005: 96)*

Technology is not mentioned here as a capability input. Of course, Sen acknowledges, as we saw, that technical artefacts like bicycles can expand human capabilities. And in some other publications he mentions that technological progress has an instrumental role to play in human development (e.g. Drèze and Sen 2002: 3). Yet until quite recently technology never received any in-depth treatment in the capability approach literature. The first specialized publication on the capability approach and technology, more specifically on ICT (information and communications technology), did already appear at the end of the 1990s (Garnham 1997). It seems, however, that up to roughly 2007 there were still fewer than a dozen other publications on the topic. These publications were moreover largely unrelated, as they were spread over different disciplines and journals. After that, there seems to have been an exponential growth of work on technology and the capability approach. An indication of this is that a bibliography compiled in early 2012 contained 79 publications that substantively engage with the topic, 91 per cent stemming from 2006 or later and 53 per cent originating from 2010 or later (Oosterlaken 2012b). This book will draw on this increasing body of literature,[9] including my own work.[10]

Useful as the capability approach may be as a normative lens through which to examine technology understood in this way, it has certain limitations. Both the benefits and limitations will be addressed at various places in the present book. However, it seems useful to discuss one major limitation right at the start, namely that – as Robeyns (2005: 94) has pointed out – the capability approach

> is not a theory that can *explain* poverty, inequality or well-being; instead, it rather provides a tool and a framework within which to *conceptualize* and *evaluate* these phenomena. Applying the capability approach to issues of policy and social change will therefore often require the addition of explanatory theories.

Likewise, the capability approach on its own is not able to explain why or when technology contributes to poverty reduction, or when it exacerbates existing inequalities. More specifically, it does not help us to understand the different ways in which technology and human capabilities are or can be related. It gives us a conceptual framework to evaluate, for example, the outcome of technological development projects. We could apply the capability approach without using work from fields like science and technology studies, design studies and philosophy of technology. This would however mean that the technology in question can and will then only be discussed in a generalizing or superficial way; it remains a black box. There would then be an important limitation on one's ability to understand the impact of a technological development project on human capabilities. One would not be able to investigate in any detail if the choice of the technology, or the way in which it was designed, or its embedding in socio-technical networks, plays an explanatory role in achieving the project outcomes. One might not even think of asking these questions, as one might not even be able to fully see their relevance.

Considering this limitation, it is not surprising that much of the recent work on technology and the capability approach have explored the compatibility of the capability approach with various theoretical perspectives on technology and engineering design. One's answer to the question of which perspectives can fruitfully supplement the capability approach will depend on one's purpose, but also on the general merits of these perspectives and theories. There is no single way to 'operationalize' the capability approach in the domain of technology and design. It should be noted though that it may not be inconsequential which supplementary technology accounts one chooses. Although making such a choice will generally speaking be unavoidable to operationalize the capability approach, it may sometimes also be a choice that is controversial. One also needs to be aware of the possibility that certain theoretical assumptions may not be compatible (Oosterlaken 2013). Throughout the book, a range of technology and design perspectives is discussed in relation to the capability approach.

Aims and structure of this book

The capability approach is a general conceptual framework, and countless different technologies exist and are applied in myriad ways. This book will provide little by way of concrete guidance for how to make any specific technology better contribute to human development. Rather, the overall aim of the book is to give the reader a solid theoretical basis to reflect on technology from the perspective of the capability approach. Although some engineers and designers may be motivated to plough through the many insightful books and articles of Sen, Nussbaum and other capability theorists, it is not realistic to expect this from all of them. It is hoped that this book will make a contribution to explaining the capability approach to this group in an accessible way. At the same time it may perhaps serve to introduce development scholars and other non-technologists to some of the complexities of making technology work for human development. More specifically, this book has four objectives. First, to examine the strengths and limitations of the capability approach as a critical lens to technology (book as a whole). Second, to put such a capability approach to technology in the context of some historical and current debates about technology and human development (Chapters 1 and 4). Third, to argue that understanding the technology–capability relationship requires iteratively 'zooming in' on the design details of technical artefacts, and 'zooming out' to the embedding of technical artefacts in socio-technical networks (Chapters 2–3). Fourth, to show that various technology and design accounts may fruitfully supplement the capability approach (book as a whole).

One way to clarify the strengths and limitations of the capability approach, which is part of the first objective of this book, would have been to extensively discuss the criticisms it has received from philosophers, economists and other scholars. These include for example the criticism that the capability approach would be too complex to apply or operationalize. It would therefore not provide a realistic alternative to the standard economic approaches and methods (Sugden 1993).[11] An example of a criticism made by a philosopher (Pogge 2002) is that the capability approach would wrongly take *all* facts of interpersonal diversity as relevant to the issue of justice, and that it would insufficiently recognize the moral relevance of the causal origins of inequalities.[12] Such general criticisms have already been debated elsewhere and a proper assessment of their strength would take too much attention away from the focus of this book: the capability approach *as a lens to technology*. Another way to get a better understanding of the strengths and limitations of the capability approach would be to contrast it with alternative general development paradigms (such as the basic needs approach) or normative frameworks (such as the human right framework). Others have already made such comparisons (see e.g. Crocker 2008; Vizard *et al.* 2011), although not specifically applied to technology. Comparing such alternative approaches and paradigms with respect to their ability to help us reflect on technology would be interesting. Yet every book has limitations in scope, and the strategy chosen for this book is to focus on giving the reader an in-depth understanding of the capability approach in relation to technology. In order to do so the book draws on different disciplines that deal with technology: design studies, science and technology studies and philosophy of technology. The focus is on how technologies change the lives of individuals. Readers who are more interested in how innovation processes more generally contribute to human development are referred to a recent book by Hartmann (2014), which connects insights from innovation economics and the capability approach.

Chapter 1 examines three different, broad and general views on poverty reduction and technology – as presented by Leach and Scoones (2006) – through the lens of the capability approach. The first view is that technologies can have a direct, worldwide impact on poverty ('the race to the universal fix'). The second view is that technologies contribute to economic competitiveness and growth, which in turn would lead to poverty reduction ('the race to the top'). The third view is one which emphasizes bottom-up, participatory technological development, taking into account varying local social, cultural and institutional realities (the so-called 'slow race'). The chapter will discuss one specific perspective that fits with the 'slow race' in more detail, namely the appropriate technology movement. This perspective on technology and development was very popular in the 1970s/1980s, and traces of its influence can still be found today. The chapter discusses what the capability approach has in common with the appropriate technology movement, but also how it could extend it. The chapter ends with a discussion about what is really core to the capability approach, and how much room this core leaves for different views on technology and human development.

Chapters 2 and 3 present a view which I have developed in previous work (Oosterlaken 2013). Arguably, both the details of design and the socio-technical embedding of technical artefacts are relevant factors in the expansion of human capabilities. Understanding the relation between technical artefacts and human capabilities therefore requires us to iteratively move back and forth between 'zooming in' and 'zooming out'. Zooming in allows us to see the specific features or details of design of technical artefacts (Chapter 2). Zooming out allows us to see how exactly technical artefacts are embedded in broader socio-technical networks and practices (Chapter 3). The capability approach is a conceptual framework that highlights certain values – especially well-being, agency and justice – and acknowledges that people may have very different yet legitimate views of the good life. These three values and the topic of the 'good life' will get explicit attention in both chapters. A connection will be made with various technology and design accounts, such as value sensitive design, participatory design, universal design, actor–network theory and pluralist versus system/network views of technology. The content of these two chapters has been substantially influenced by contemporary work in the field of philosophy and ethics of technology. Unfortunately there is presently still hardly any empirical work available which could serve to illustrate the ideas presented in these chapters in great detail. The emphasis is on making the connection between ideas in the capability approach and in a number of technology and design accounts. It is my hope though that these chapters will inspire further, more practical work and real-world applications in the future. Chapters 2 and 3 are, in contrast to Chapters 1 and 4, not specifically focused on the global South – although some examples from a developing country context will feature in them. There is actually nothing in the capability approach that limits its application to contexts of poverty reduction and underdevelopment, and a considerable part of the capability approach literature indeed describes applications in the global North, or discusses issues that pertain worldwide. This also applies to the sub-body of literature on technology and the capability approach. For example, it has been used to discuss normative issues with respect to the design and implementation of robots to solve the problems of rising costs and personnel shortage in Western health care (Borenstein and Pearson 2010; Coeckelbergh 2012). There is furthermore no reason why reflection on technology in the global South could not, just like reflection on technology in the global North, benefit from a thorough theoretical basis. To a large degree this basis could be the same.

Chapter 4 does focus on the global South again, as it discusses the application of the capability approach in the domain of ICT for Development (ICT4D). It starts out with a discussion on whether there is anything special about ICTs, which would set them apart from earlier technologies which were introduced in developing countries. The next section will discuss various ways in which 'mainstream' ICT4D has been criticized from the perspective of the capability approach. The third section of the chapter discusses a case study, namely a project in which mp3 players and podcasts were introduced in a rural area in Zimbabwe. One of the attractive features of this case is that it illustrates the importance of both 'zooming in' and 'zooming out'. The fourth section pays particular attention to the values of well-being and agency in ICT4D initiatives, and the tension that may arise between them. This is done on the basis of the podcasting example and that of the telecentres. The latter are public ICT centres, for example in rural areas

Figure 0.2 The technology–capability relationship: 'zooming in' and 'zooming out'

where private ICT access is still low, where people can go to use computers. The last section of Chapter 4 discusses the various ways in which the capability approach might be operationalized and used within ICT4D, with the aim of further illustrating the versatility of the approach.

Notes

1 Despite many commonalities between their writings on the capability approach, Sen and Nussbaum have each applied and developed the approach in their own way. For a discussion of the differences between their views on the capability approach, see e.g. Robeyns (2005) and part II of Crocker (2008). This book is to a large degree based on the work of Nussbaum, but will at various places also draw on the work of Sen.
2 Of course there are both practical and normative limitations to such freedom. Normative limitations arise, for example, as a consequence of issues of sustainability and intergenerational justice, and from the need to equally respect the freedom of others.
3 For a general, introductory textbook on the capability approach, and the human development approach more broadly, the reader is referred to Deneulin and Shahani (2009). A good introduction to the capability approach from a philosophical perspective is provided by Robeyns (2011).
4 See the film *Wadjda* (2012), written and directed by Haifaa Al Mansour, about a young girl in Saudi Arabia who wishes to cycle. Two months after the movie appeared, Al Mansour narrates in an interview that cycling became partially allowed for women. They are still not allowed to use bicycles as a means of transport in the city, but they can now use bicycles in parks for recreational purposes – provided that they are dressed decently and accompanied by a male relative while cycling (Bockting, 2012).
5 This example of washing powder was introduced by the philosopher Bernard William (1987) in response to Sen's work.
6 www.coop-africa.org/en/what-we-do/bike4care/265-health-workers-in-kisumu-kenya (accessed 19 January 2013).
7 In his historical study of bicycle development in nineteenth-century Europe Bijker (1995) shows that here as well – just as in Saudi Arabia – cultural norms were such that women were initially not allowed to use bicycles. He finds (p. 22) that in Europe 'the first cycles in fact reinforced the existing "gender order"', while they 'later became an instrument for women's emancipation'. See also Macy (2011).
8 This section is a revised version of a section in Oosterlaken (forthcoming).
9 For an extensive overview of the literature up to 2012, see Oosterlaken (2012a).
10 One limitation of the book is that it is based solely on literature in the English language, even though it is to be expected that relevant literature has also appeared in other languages. In Latin America, for example, there is a quite active network of capability scholars and some of them may have used it to reflect on technology.

Introduction **17**

11 For a discussion of this criticism, see Robeyns (2000).
12 For a critical analysis of and reply to Pogge's criticism, see Oosterlaken (2013b).

References

Alkire, S. (2005a). Capability and Functionings: Definition and Justification. In: *Briefing Notes (last updated 1 September 2005)*. Human Development and Capability Association.
Alkire, S. (2005b). Why the Capability Approach? *Journal of Human Development* 6(1):115–33.
Bijker, W.E. (1995). *Of Bicycles, Bakelites, and Bulbs; Toward a Theory of Sociotechnical Change*. Cambridge, MA: MIT Press.
Bockting, B.J. (2012). Krassen binnen de lijnen. In: *De Volkskrant*. Amsterdam.
Borenstein, J., and Pearson, Y. (2010). Robot Caregivers: Harbingers of Expanded Freedom for All? *Ethics and Information Technology* 12(4):277–88.
Coeckelbergh, M. (2012). 'How I Learned to Love the Robot': Capabilities, Information Technologies, and Elderly Care. In: Oosterlaken, I. and Van den Hoven, J. (eds), *The Capability Approach, Technology & Design*. Dordrecht: Springer.
Crocker, D.A. (2008). *Ethics of Global Development: Agency, Capability, and Deliberative Democracy*. Cambridge: Cambridge University Press.
Crocker, D.A., and Robeyns, I. (2010). Capability and Agency. In: Morris, C.W. (ed.), *Amartya Sen*. Cambridge: Cambridge University Press.
Deneulin, S. and Shahani, L. (eds) (2009). *An Introduction to the Human Development and Capability Approach*. Ottawa: Earthscan/IDRC.
Drèze, J. and Sen, A. (2002). *India: Development and Participation*. Oxford: Oxford University Press.
Garnham, N. (1997). Amartya Sen's 'Capability' Approach to the Evaluation of Welfare: Its Application to Communications. *Javnost – The Public* 4(4):25–34.
Hanlon, J. and Smart, T. (2008). *Do Bicycles Equal Development in Mozambique?* Rochester, NY and Woodbridge: James Currey.
Hartmann, D. (2014). *Economic Complexity and Human Development: How Economic Diversification and Social Networks Affect Human Agency and Welfare*. New York: Routledge.
Leach, M. and Scoones, I. (2006). *The Slow Race: Making Technology Work for the Poor*. London: Demos.
Macy, S. (2011). *Wheels of Change: How Women Rode the Bicycle to Freedom (with a Few Flat Tires along the Way)*. Washington, DC: National Geographic Society.
Mitcham, C. and Schatzberg, E. (2009). Defining Technology and the Engineering Sciences. In: Meijers, A. (ed.), *Philosophy of Technology and Engineering Sciences*. Amsterdam: Elsevier, pp. 27–64.
Muralidharan, K. and Prakash, N. (2013). Cycling to School: Increasing Secondary School Enrollment for Girls in India. In: *NBER Working Paper Series*. National Bureau of Economic Research, Cambridge, MA.
Nussbaum, M.C. (2000). *Women and Human Development: The Capability Approach*. New York: Cambridge University Press.

Nussbaum, M.C. (2011). *Creating Capabilities: The Human Development Approach*. Cambridge, MA: Belknap Press of Harvard University Press.
Oosterlaken, I. (2012a). The Capability Approach and Technology: Taking Stock and Looking Ahead. In: Oosterlaken, I. and Van den Hoven, J. (eds), *The Capability Approach, Technology and Design*. Dordrecht: Springer, pp. 3–26.
Oosterlaken, I. (2012b). Introduction: 'The Capability Approach and Innovation/Technology/Design'. *Maitreyee, the e-bulletin of the Human Development and Capability Association* March 2012 (special issue on innovation, technology and design).
Oosterlaken, I. (2013a). Taking a capability approach to technology and its design – a philosophical exploration (doctoral dissertation), vol. 8, Simon Stevin Series in the Ethics of Technology (edited by Brey, Philip, Kroes, Peter, Meijers, Anthonie). 3TU.Centre for Ethics and Technology, Delft.
Oosterlaken, I. (2013b). Is Pogge a Capability Theorist in Disguise? A Critical Examination of Thomas Pogge's Defence of Rawlsian Resourcism. *Ethical Theory and Moral Practice*, 16(1):205–15.
Oosterlaken, I. (forthcoming). Towards an Ethics of Technology and Human Development. In: Murphy, C., Gardoni, P., Harris, E., Hassan, B. and Eyad, M. (eds), *Engineering Ethics in a Globalized World*. Dordrecht: Springer.
Pogge, T. (2002). Can the Capability Approach Be Justified? *Philosophical Topics*, 30(2):167–228.
Robeyns, I. (2000). An Unworkable Idea or a Promising Alternative? Sen's Capability Approach Re-examined. *Center for Economic Studies Discussion paper 00.30*. Leuven: Katholieke Universiteit Leuven.
Robeyns, I. (2005). The Capability Approach – A Theoretical Survey. *Journal of Human Development*, 6(1):94–114.
Robeyns, I. (2006). The Capability Approach in Practice. *Journal of Political Philosophy* 14(3):351–76.
Robeyns, I. (2011). The Capability Approach. In: Zalta, E. N. (ed), *Stanford Encyclopedia of Philosophy*.
Sen, A. (1979). Equality of What? In: *The Tanner Lecture on Human Values*. Delivered at Stanford University, 22 May.
Sen, A. (1983). Poor, Relatively Speaking. *Oxford Economic Papers (New Series)* 35(2):153–69.
Sen, A. (1985). *Commodities and Capabilities*. Amsterdam & New York: North-Holland.
Sen, A. (1987). *On Ethics and Economics*. Oxford: Basil Blackwell.
Sen, A. (1999). *Development as Freedom*. New York: Anchor Books.
Sugden, R. (1993). Welfare, Resources, and Capabilities: A Review of Inequality Reexamined by Amartya Sen. *Journal of Economic Literature* 31:1947–62.
Vizard, P., Fukuda-Parr, S. and Elson, D. (2011). Introduction: The Capability Approach and Human Rights. *Journal of Human Development and Capabilities* 12(1):1–22.
Williams, B. (1987). The Standard of Living: Interests and Capabilities. In: G. Hawthorn (ed.), *The Standard of Living* [Sen's 1985 Tanner Lectures at Cambridge, with comments by various authors]. Cambridge: Cambridge University Press.

1
THE APPROPRIATE TECHNOLOGY MOVEMENT AND THE CAPABILITY APPROACH[1]

Technology as a universal fix, economic driver, or ... ?

Some years back, development scholars Melissa Leach and Ian Scoones (2006) published a pamphlet entitled *The Slow Race – Making Technology Work for the Poor*. It is very helpful as a first introduction to the possible relations between technology and poverty reduction, because it abstracts away from specific disciplinary approaches and all sorts of detailed differences of opinion that one may have about the subject. It sketches three very broad and general views on the relationship between these two phenomena (poverty reduction and technology). They label these three views as the 'race to the top', the 'race to the universal fix' and the 'slow race'. These three races, Leach and Scoones note, are not mutually exclusive and each has a role to play in human development. Yet the first two are, they observe, very prominently present in policy debates, whereas the third 'less glamorous, but ultimately more important race is being overlooked' (p. 12). I will argue in this chapter that the capability approach as a conceptual framework has a lot to offer to those wishing to criticize fixation on the first two races, and to promote the slow race instead. However, work falling into the slow race category is not beyond criticism, and I will furthermore argue that the capability approach may be used to evaluate and extend such work. This will be done by discussing one prominent example of the slow race perspective, namely the appropriate technology (AT) movement, in more detail. More specifically, it will be examined how this movement deals with the value of agency and with gender issues, and what perspective the capability approach has to offer on these topics. Moreover, I will argue in the last sections of this chapter that it would be premature to conclude that the capability approach is not at all compatible with the other two 'races'. What is needed is a more extensive, nuanced discussion of different strategies for making technology contribute to poverty reduction.

Let us first discuss each of the three races in turn. The 'race to the top' refers to 'the top in the global economy'. According to this view, science and technology are essential to be able to compete in the global economy and to create economic growth. It is in line with the classical post-Second World War view of development as modernization, Leach and Scoones (p. 12) note, 'presuming that developing countries will move through a series of stages towards industrial and post-industrial glory'. Poverty reduction occurs, in this view, by this 'science and technology driven economic growth' trickling down to the poor. Leach and Scoones mention a UN Millennium Report (Juma and Yee-Cheong 2005) as an illustration, but the 2001 report of the UN Development Programme could also have served as an example. The UNDP's annual Human Development Report highlights a different theme each year, and in 2001 this was technology. Listing some of the key terms of the report (UNDP 2001) gives you an immediate feel for how this report fits to a large extent in with this perspective of a race to the top: scientific progress, diffusion of technology, investments, risks, patents, globalization, age of the network, skilled labour force, advanced skills ... Despite having been published over a decade ago, the language of this report still sounds very relevant today.

It is generally accepted that technological progress plays a key role in economic growth, and that economic growth can in turn contribute to poverty reduction. However, it is equally clear that the latter will not always and without exception be the case. In the last decades of the twentieth century many developing countries had substantial growth rates, but some economists argue that the absolute number of people living in poverty was still on the rise (Thirwall 2008). Economic growth is therefore a poor indicator of development, as is income per capita of well-being. Furthermore, the total set of goods and services may grow, but what the impact will be on the lives of people living in poverty also depends on the composition and distribution of this set. The way in which technological modernization and economic growth are pursued may even harm already vulnerable and marginalized groups. Projects introducing a large dam in a developing country have in the past had such negative effects (see e.g. Roy 1999). The capability approach could be used to analyse such cases, as it is committed to treating each person as an end in themselves (Nussbaum 2000: 55–9); it takes an interest in the capabilities of each and every individual to lead the life they have reason to value. Capability scholars are therefore inclined to be careful with relying on group averages. They would also tend to be critical of sacrificing the capabilities of individuals to 'non-capability collective goals' (Robeyns 2014: 14) such as growth or modernization. As for the composition of economic production: science and technology may enable a country to start producing cheap vaccines for common diseases, but also weapons. Both could contribute equally to economic growth, but their impact on people's quality of life will be quite different. The capability approach may be very helpful in voicing such criticisms on 'the race to the top' because – as was explained in the Introduction – it asks exactly this question of how to assess societal change, and argues that this should not be done in terms of income or production, but rather in terms of the capability set of each and every person.

The 'race to the universal fix', Leach and Scoones say, focuses – contrary to the 'race to the top' – directly on poverty. It promotes looking for 'breakthroughs in science and technology that will have a direct and widespread impact on poverty', those 'big-hitting technologies with the potential for global scope and application' (p. 13). Whereas in the past this view inspired public investments in science and R&D, nowadays – so these authors notice – this view is mainly promoted and implemented by public–private sector collaborations. They see the work done by the Bill and Melinda Gates Foundation as an exemplification of this view. This foundation invests, for example, a lot of money in research into diseases that seriously affect many of the income-poor in the global South, such as malaria. Leach and Scoones quote the website of the foundation as saying that they are looking for effective solutions which can be produced against low costs and then easily distributed worldwide.[2] This view is also present in the 2001 UNDP report, which claims that 'the 20th century's unprecedented gains in advancing human development and eradicating poverty came largely from technological breakthroughs' (p. 2 of the overview of the report). Examples mentioned by the report are the potential of new medicines and crop varieties.

Leach and Scoones see several problems with the 'race to the universal fix'. One of these is that 'ecologies and the practices that people have developed to sustain their livelihoods are highly diverse' (p. 22). Technological solutions, they claim, must be appropriate to these particular local circumstances. And sometimes it may be best to adapt 'old' technologies, which have already proved their value, to fit these circumstances. As was argued in the Introduction, an awareness of human diversity pervades the capability approach literature. More concretely, when zooming in on the relation between technological artefacts and human capabilities this human diversity enters the analysis as so-called 'conversion factors'. Furthermore, Leach and Scoones note, the 'problems of poverty, hunger and illness are not just the result of technical matters' (p. 23). These problems also have other causes, such as conflicts and market failures. Moreover, social, technical and political aspects tend to be closely intertwined. They give the example of large-scale irrigation technologies, which to many seem to be the best solution to the apparently objective problem of water scarcity. But it is politics that determines whose water needs are addressed – e.g. of farmers, industries or consumers. And it partly depends on local institutions and regulations what the impact of a water technology is. Thus it is dangerous they conclude to look for the 'best' technological solution without also taking into account non-technical aspects. If one focuses so single-mindedly on technology as a universal fix for poverty, one could be said to have fallen prey to 'technology fetishism'. Especially engineers might be said to be vulnerable to this affliction,[3] with their keen interest in 'new' technologies. This recalls Amartya Sen (1984, 1985) accusing economists of suffering, all too often, from 'commodity fetishism'. One of the advantages of the capability approach is, according to Robeyns (2011), that it proposes to focus on the ultimate ends of development: those individual capabilities that enable people to lead flourishing human lives; 'By starting from ends, we do not a priori assume that there is only one overridingly important means to that ends (such as income)', she notices (p. 12), 'but rather explicitly ask the question which types of means are important for the fostering and nurturing of a particular capability, or set of capabilities'. Those means may or may not include technology.

The third possible relationship between technology and poverty, the so-called 'slow race', is actually not a race at all. It is about making sure that technology fits the local context. It is furthermore a view which recognizes (p. 14) that 'technological fixes are not enough, and that social, cultural and institutional dimensions are also key'. It emphasizes the importance of bottom-up, participatory processes and sees a central role for citizens in technology choice, engineering design and the implementation and regulation of technology. This is according to Leach and Scoones in sharp contrast with the previous two views, where people are being viewed as 'passive beneficiaries of trickle-down development or technology transfer' (p. 14). Illustrative of this 'slow race' perspective is the fierce criticism of Vandana Shiva (2001), an Indian activist, in the 2001 UNDP report. She argues that 'human concerns' and ecology are largely overlooked in this report, and that it pays insufficient attention to the importance of people's participation, and to the diversity of technological solutions available worldwide. According to Shiva the debate about technology should also embrace cultural diversity, which can be a stimulus for innovation. Yet she finds the report ignores the active role of the global South in processes of technological change. She criticizes the report's apparent assumption that 'new' technology is always better than existing or past ways of doing things. Furthermore, she is disappointed that the UNDP apparently ascribes to the much criticized view of technological determinism,[4] in the sense that it assumes that 'technology shapes society [and not also the other way around] and technological change is always positive and progressive'. Determining whether her criticism is fully justified would require a more thorough discussion of the report, but the criticism does illustrate the sort of concerns that the 'slow race' perspective would raise.

From these three perspectives on the relation between technology and poverty reduction, the 'slow race' seems to be the one that is best aligned with the capability approach. Why is this the case? One reason is that in the 'slow race' perspective human diversity is, just like in the capability approach, recognized as being significant and far-reaching. Furthermore the 'slow race' and the capability approach have in common that they put people and their lives central. The emphasis of the 'slow race' on participation and seeing people as active agents in technological change also dovetails nicely with the oeuvre of Sen and the emphasis that he put on agency (as discussed in the Introduction). Leach and Scoones mention among others the appropriate technology (AT) movement as being one of the approaches falling into this category of the 'slow race'. The next section will discuss this movement in some detail, and subsequently explore in more depth how the capability approach relates to it.

The appropriate technology movement

The AT movement arose as a response to attempts in the 1950s and 1960s to achieve quick development results by means of the transfer of modern technology from the global North to the global South. In that way developing countries could, so it was expected, take shortcuts from the economic development path that wealthy nations had followed in the past. For a variety of reasons many people became over time disappointed with this strategy. The capital-intensive production methods that were transferred did not create the jobs that the income-poor needed so much. Still many people started to migrate from the rural areas to the cities, against all odds hoping to find a job and a better life. The slums that arose intensified the problems that developing countries faced. In the rural areas meanwhile agriculture and traditional industries faced a rapid decline, and social disruption aggravated poverty. Environmental pollution also became an issue. In the 1970s university research centres and development organizations started to work on alternative technologies and strategies. One of the most influential figures in the AT movement was Schumacher, who in 1973 published his book *Small Is Beautiful: A Study of Economics As If People Mattered*. His thinking was influenced by various traditions, one of which was that of 'Indian community development' as initiated by Gandhi. The AT movement paid attention to both production technologies, hence those contributing to economic development, and technologies directly meeting human needs (Willoughby 1990). It thus provides an alternative to both the race to the top and the race to the universal fix. Although the AT movement as such lost momentum after the early 1980s, many of its ideas have survived and have heavily influenced more recent discourses (Nieusma and Riley 2010), such as currently on 'technology for social inclusion' in Latin America (Smith *et al*. 2014). It is therefore still interesting to look at this movement in order to get a better grip on the meaning, relevance and limitations of the capability approach in the context of technology. The relation between ideas in the AT movement and in the capability approach has been discussed by Fernández-Baldor *et al*. (2012, 2014) and Oosterlaken *et al*. (2012).[5] As it happens, both refer to a case study of a recent project by Practical Action, a development organization that specializes in technology and is historically rooted in the AT movement. The cases discussed in Fernández-Baldor *et al*. (2012, 2014) concern projects introducing energy technologies in rural areas of Bolivia, Guatemala and Peru. The case discussed in Oosterlaken *et al*. (2012) is a project introducing mp3 players in a rural area of Zimbabwe. This chapter will briefly address both cases, and the case from Oosterlaken *et al*. (2012) will be discussed more extensively in Chapter 4.

So what is this AT movement about? According to Willoughby (1990) even within the movement there is disagreement and a lack of clarity about the meaning of appropriate technology. He sees this as one of the reasons that 'while becoming a significant international movement Appropriate Technology has remained a minority theme within technology policy and practices' (p. 12). It is indeed hard to characterize this rather heterogeneous movement in a few words, and no generalization will do justice to all initiatives and views within the movement. Nieusma (2004: 13) summarizes the ideas behind the AT movement as follows:

> In part as a response to failures of technology transfer approaches, 'appropriate technologists' argued that context suitability should be central to identifying technologies relevant to poor people of the Third World and other marginalized social groups ... Attention to contextual particularities became one of the guiding approaches to appropriate technology and, hence, unlike technology transfer scholars, appropriate technology thinking took design as the point of intervention.

The idea is that it depends on the details of design whether a technology is suitable for a certain context. Whether it concerns energy technologies, agricultural technologies or other types of technology – there is according to this view no reason to assume that the most 'modern' or 'advanced' technology is always the best option. However, it is of course also not true that just any technological alternative will do. When designing a new technical artefact our design requirements should be context specific. This focus on the details of design does not mean that applying appropriate technology always requires a bespoke design solution. It may also mean that the design features of an existing technological artefact play a central role in the choice to adopt it in a specific context of application.

Nieusma's explanation of appropriate technology is an example of what Willoughby (1990, 2005) calls the 'general principles approach' to appropriate technology. This conceptualization of appropriate technology leads to a rather formal definition of the movement, namely that it emphasizes 'the universal importance of examining the appropriateness of technology in each set of circumstances', while keeping in sight the ends that one wishes to achieve (Willoughby 2005: 21). It thus stays close to the everyday meaning of the adjective 'appropriate'; something – a technological artefact in this case – is always appropriate for something else. Such appropriateness may have many different dimensions, thus according to this approach we should always ask: 'appropriate for what?' Take the case of the mp3 players introduced by Practical Action in a rural area in Zimbabwe (Oosterlaken *et al.* 2012). This case – which will be discussed in more detail in Chapter 4 – shows that a technology may be culturally appropriate, as when loudspeakers instead of headphones are added to an mp3 player in order to enable collective listening in line with African community practices. It may be appropriate for specific user groups, as when a choice is made for a voice-based technology in an area with a lot of illiteracy. It may be appropriate for an area lacking certain infrastructure, as solar-powered mp3 devices may be for an area without an electricity network. And technology may be appropriate in an economic, political, ecological or other sense. The important thing to note is that the general principle does not define a specific type of appropriateness, it just claims that appropriateness – whether culturally, socially, environmentally or economically – is a very important consideration in all our dealings with technology.

Willoughby (2005) distinguishes this 'general principles approach' from the 'specific characteristics approach', which was according to him prevalent within the movement. In this second understanding appropriate technology is given a fixed and specific interpretation, for example an appropriate technology should be ecologically sound, easy to use, low cost, low maintenance, labour intensive, energy efficient, etc. Labour-intensive technologies would for example be more appropriate for developing countries due to the fact that in those countries capital is relatively scarce, whereas labour is abundantly available and therefore relatively cheap. Waged labour is also a potential way for people to earn an income and escape from poverty, which would make labour-intensive technologies in principle desirable for developing countries. According to Willoughby (2005: 21) the specific-characteristics definition of appropriateness:

> is more than a concept about the nature of technology and the way it relates to ends. It is simultaneously a normative statement (because it assumes priority for certain ends rather than others) and an empirical statement (because the practical criteria of appropriateness must be based upon some assessment of which technical means generally best serve the ends in question). Whereas the general-principles approach tends to leave the evaluation of ends and means relatively open, the specific-characteristics approach embodies the results of previous efforts to evaluate both of these factors.

Of course, the capability approach would ascribe one important normative goal to technology, namely the expansion of valuable human capabilities – although it would certainly not claim that this should be the only goal. But especially if one keeps it an open question which capabilities should be promoted – as Sen does – the capability approach seems perfectly compatible with the 'general principles approach' to appropriate technology. The role and value that the capability approach ascribes to agency arguably even implies that the 'general principles approach' is to be preferred over a 'specific characteristics approach' to appropriate technology. After all, the latter leaves less room for communities to decide for themselves which ends to pursue and which means to select.

Another reason to be hesitant to embrace a 'specific characteristics approach' is that there seems to be an implicit assumption that developing countries all share certain characteristics that make certain technologies more appropriate for them than others. Such an assumption would be in line with a key developmental paradigm during the early decades of development cooperation, namely 'the essentialization of the Third World and its inhabitants as homogeneous entities' (Schuurman 2008: 15). If this were to be taken to the extreme and applied to the issue of technology, the distinction between 'appropriate technology' and the 'race to the universal fix' would become blurry. It might then be assumed, for example, that some low-maintenance, labour-intensive technological solution is best for each and every developing country. Since the early 1980s, however, development scholars have increasingly questioned the assumption that all developing countries are alike. New studies have instead revealed 'the growing diversity of (under)development experiences' (Schuurman 2008: 13). Capability scholars also tend to emphasize human diversity over and over again in their work – not only between developing countries, but also between regions, between different groups in any region, and between persons within any group (such as 'the poor'). As was explained in the Introduction, the fact of immense human diversity is one of the main reasons why the capability approach proposes to focus on the expansion of valuable human capabilities instead of access to resources as the end of development. After all, 'conversion factors' may be such that a certain technology does not lead to the same expansion of human capabilities for every person in every context. What getting access to electricity does for the capabilities of a person will for example depend on which sort of electrical appliances are locally within reach. And in a situation where computer skills are largely absent, people will benefit less than they potentially could have from getting access to the internet. The same is true if locally relevant online content is lacking. While these examples may sound like kicking at an open door, in reality there is often a multitude of such factors at play – some of which are less obvious than others. Of course no project or policy is able to deal with all factors of human diversity simultaneously, therefore discussion and judgement is always needed on which factors matter most in specific cases or in relation to specific capabilities.

Although no specific interpretation of the concept 'appropriate technology' will reflect the diversity which exists within and between developing countries, the AT movement was in practice still quite heterogeneous. Within this movement many different technological solutions were developed and promoted by a range of different organizations. It challenged the idea that modern, high-tech solutions are always best, and this opened the door for more critical reflection on technology and development. In other words, it has promoted the insight that one should evaluate the appropriateness of any technology for the circumstances that apply and the ends that are chosen. With the AT movement, one could say, a start was made with taking 'conversion factors' seriously – even though this specific concept was not used at the time. If one is interested in expanding valuable human capabilities with the help of technology, one may therefore benefit from the work that has been done by people and organizations within, or influenced by, the AT movement. Thanks to this movement there exists a great diversity of technological solutions and a wealth of knowledge about why these would be appropriate for certain circumstances (see e.g. Hazeltine and Bull 1999). At the same time, proponents of appropriate technology may have something to gain from the capability approach as well. According to Willoughby (1990: 13) a significant reason for the limited long-term influence of the movement would appear to lie with the lack of a clearly articulated formal theory, the salient features of which are both universally recognized by the movement and identifiable by those outside the movement. It is to such a theoretical framework that the capability approach, as a general conceptual framework with universal appeal, may be able to contribute something. More specifically, its contribution would lie in providing the ends that can be used to assess whether a technology is appropriate enough, and whether it is ultimately a success – namely the sustainable expansion of valuable individual capabilities, so that people are empowered to lead the lives they have reason to value. Focusing on capability expansion as the ultimate goal in one's evaluations, instead of on the instrumental goal of a sustainable implementation of the technology, may also be helpful in that it is more likely to draw attention to the indirect mechanisms through which new technologies may affect people's lives.

Beyond appropriate technology: agency

The capability approach and the AT movement may thus be said to have something in common, namely their emphasis on the fact of human diversity and its importance for evaluating technological resources. However, it has also been argued that adopting a capability approach of technology would go substantially beyond taking the approach of the AT movement. The two issues at stake are gender and agency. In Sen's work, Crocker and Robeyns (2010) argue, agency is valued in three ways. First, respecting agency has *instrumental* value, as taking the perspective of local people into account increases the chances of development projects being successful. Second, respecting agency is *constructively* valuable, since in the process of exercising his agency, a person 'scrutinizes, decides on, and shapes its values' (p. 83), in interaction with others. And last but not least, agency has *intrinsic* value, meaning that it is valuable for its own sake and not just as a means towards some end.

The issue of agency and appropriate technology is extensively discussed by Fernández-Baldor *et al.* (2012). They illustrate their argument with three cases of introducing a micro hydro power plant in a rural area in Latin America. It concerns a small installation that produces electricity from a natural water flow, such as a nearby waterfall or stream. According to Practical Action it is a form of appropriate technology, as it 'provides poor communities in rural areas with an affordable, easy to maintain and long-term solution to their energy needs'.[6] The first project, in a rural area in Bolivia, is a classic case of a failed technological development project. The community is hardly involved in the design and construction phase, and sometime after implementation the plant experiences maintenance problems, for which nobody is willing or able to take responsibility – in the end leading to frequent interruptions of power. In the second case, in the same area, micro hydro power was implemented through a strong participatory process. The plant is still operational and has led to a variety of well-being improvements for the community. People's capability to have good health was for example improved because of a reduction in indoor smoke now that electric light is available. And the latter has also increased conditions for studying, thus an expansion of the capability to be educated took place. This is the same in the third case, in a rural area in Guatemala, but in addition here (p. 145) 'the project has served as a driving force for the community to become involved in other new projects …The success of the first project (electrification) led the community to believe in their ability to face new challenges'. New initiatives not only served the interests of participants, but also included actions for the greater good of the community.

Although Fernández-Baldor *et al.* (2012) appreciate the expansion of individual capabilities that resulted from the second energy project, they argue that development projects should ideally, like the third energy project, also be 'instruments for promoting and supporting complex processes of change and transformation' (p. 136). To support their argument and conceptualize this different way of looking at technological development projects Fernández-Baldor *et al.* (2012) invoke the capability approach – and especially the concept of agency as discussed by Sen. The AT movement, they acknowledge, already promoted community participation. Yet they judge that this was done in a limited and instrumental way, by providing information to local people and consulting them in so far as needed to make a choice for an appropriate technology and achieve the project's end – a sustainable implementation of the technology. In their view communities themselves should be in the driving seat of technological development projects, which should reflect their values and goals. Moreover, the focus should be on the process of transformation, rather than on a limited set of ends directly related to the function of the technology in question. In other words – processes are also important as outcomes, and more emphasis should be put on the constructive and intrinsic value of agency. Some capability scholars have argued that collective action is often a powerful means for improving the lives of the income poor (Ibrahim 2006; Stewart 2005). Agreeing with this, Fernández-Baldor *et al.* (2012) discuss both individual and collective agency.

An interesting question is of course when exactly a technological development project has a transformative effect, by increasing collective and individual agency. Which factors or conditions does one need to focus on to achieve this result? Technology choice might be one factor here. A later publication by the same authors (Fernández-Baldor *et al.* 2014) looks into four different energy projects, implemented by Practical Action in Peru. Two projects implemented micro hydro power, one a micro wind network and one project combined individual solar power and wind energy. As the technology is simpler in the last two cases, these were mainly implemented by Practical Action technicians, with limited attention being paid to community participation. The two hydro power projects required extensive community contributions to creating the required infrastructure, which seems – so the authors postulate – to have contributed to 'building a sense of community' (p. 22). Yet given that the three micro hydro power plants projects – discussed above – differed in their transformative effect despite using a similar technology, Fernández-Baldor *et al.* acknowledge that technology choice is clearly not decisive.

It should be noted at this point that participatory development has been on the agenda of development organizations since the mid 1970s, and even became the new 'mantra' at a certain point (Mohan 2008). Yet as we saw, development scholars like Leach and Scoones (2006) still notice insufficient attention for participation and respect for people's agency when it comes to discourses on and practices of technology and development. Moreover, the definition of participation and the underlying reasons for applying it in development have been contested. Furthermore major problems have surfaced over time (Mohan 2008). One problem mentioned by Mohan is tokenism, where participation is more rhetoric than about actual empowerment. The capability approach as a mere conceptual framework cannot take away the real-world causes – whatever they may be – of the limited implementation of the ideals of participatory development. It may however play a role in our critical reflection on the issue, including analysing and criticizing existing practices. Mohan (pp. 48–9) draws attention to the problem that 'for the poor their lack of resources means that any participatory process must yield tangible benefits. In turn, this forces us to consider people not as idealized political subjects, but as embodied agents, shaped and constrained by material and cultural structures.' The capability approach does exactly that, as a 'comprehensive and holistic approach' (Robeyns 2011: 9) which considers agency in relation to people's capability set, which in turn depends on such structures (which will be discussed further in Chapter 3). Another problem is, Mohan says (p. 48), that 'much participatory development has treated communities as socially homogeneous', for example not paying attention to power or gender differences. Considering its acknowledgement of the salience of human diversity, the capability approach could again make a contribution. Frediani (2007: 3) notes similar problems as Mohan with participatory development practice, and argues that participatory methods need to be combined with an approach that facilitates an exploration of 'the nature of people's lives and the relations between the many dimensions of well-being'. This approach, he says, should be comprehensive, but flexible and able to capture complex linkages between (aspects of) poverty, intervention, participation and empowerment. He feels that the capability approach is able to offer exactly that.[7]

Appropriate for whom? Gender and technology

Of the three broad and general categories of conversion factors distinguished by Sen, it seems that the AT movement originally paid most attention to social and environmental factors. Human diversity at the level of individuals, and related differences in personal conversion factors, received less attention. As Lucena *et al.* (2010: 15) argue, unavoidably one arrives at a point where technical systems need to be embedded in local circumstances — which makes it inevitable that engineers have to deal with local communities and the people that make up those communities. They note that engineers have difficulties engaging with communities, due to a number of barriers. One of these is a dominant belief that 'communities are homogeneous entities that can be treated as a client or customer in a for-profit relationship or in design for industry projects' (p. 16). Lucena *et al.* discuss internal differences between people as one of the 'key characteristics of community' that engineers have to reckon with, and this resonates with the emphasis that the capability approach puts on interpersonal diversity. Relevant dimensions of such diversity may be identified by an exercise of thinking through how the intended technological project affects the capability set of different categories of people in different ways.

Gender is of course only one dimension of interpersonal diversity, and the focus on gender in this section should not be taken to mean that others are not relevant in the context of technology and poverty reduction. Yet the available literature facilitates using gender as an illustration of how the capability approach may supplement and extend the AT movement. Moreover, gender differences are in fact often a salient dimension of interpersonal diversity within communities. Despite this salience it was, however, not until the 1980s that the relation between gender and technology became a distinct topic of research (Stamp 1989; Suchman 2008). One of the issues around which, according to Stamp (1989: 50), some consensus emerged early on is that 'appropriate technology ... is often inappropriate when gender issues are taken into account'. One example is 'a water pump brought to the Sudan which was unusable by women because it required the operator to straddle it, which no self-respecting Sudanese woman would do' (Hazeltine and Bull 1999: 303). Another example is that 'many stoves ... require women to cook and serve food in the daylight at the expense of other tasks, as there is no longer firelight to see by' (Stamp 1989: 59). Part of the issue is of course the question of 'who decides what technology is appropriate, and whose interests does it serve?' (Stamp 1989: 50) – and there is thus a relation with the aforementioned issue of power differences and participation. Gender has been a prominent issue in development policy and practice for some decades now, and also AT organizations like Practical Action nowadays pay attention to it (Scott and Foster 2008). Yet it remains a challenge to recognize and deal with the gender issues that are at stake. For example, the case study of the mp3 players introduced by Practical Action in Zimbabwe (Oosterlaken *et al.* 2012) revealed that women were less able to benefit from the cattle management lessons recorded on podcasts. One reason was that – in line with existing cultural practices – the practice arose of listening collectively to podcasts. Existing cultural practices also meant, however, that women were always seated 'second row' in community meetings. The case study revealed that the sound volume of the mp3 players plus loudspeakers was regularly insufficient for all women to hear the lesson played. This gender issue was not picked up and addressed during the project.

The capability approach, as a normative conceptual framework, may be helpful in conceptualizing and analysing such gender issues. Gender has in fact received much attention from capability scholars, including Sen (1995) and Nussbaum (2000). The evaluative framework that the capability approach provides is according to Robeyns (2008) in several ways sensitive to gender issues. First, its focus on capabilities and functionings is helpful. Sen (1992: 125) claims that 'the question of gender inequality ... can be understood much better by comparing those things that intrinsically matter (such as functionings and capabilities), rather than just the means [to achieve them] like ... resources. The issue of gender inequality is ultimately one of disparate freedoms.' It is also important, says Robeyns (p. 89), that the capability approach also looks at people's capabilities and functionings in nonmarket settings, which many feminist economists support. The second relevant feature is the attention for human diversity – conversion factors may be very different for women and for men. The third relevant aspect is the ethical individualism of the capability approach – it makes a normative claim that each and every person should have certain capabilities. Such individualism, says Robeyns (2008: 92), 'is necessary for women and children to be given their due right and not to be subsumed under the cover of the well-being of the household, family, clan or community'. At the same time the capability approach does not subscribe to ontological or methodological individualism (Robeyns 2005: 107–10), meaning that it recognizes that humans are per definition socially embedded creatures, and should be studied as such. On the one hand this social embedding has an influence on the choices that women make (or not make, possibly as a result of adaptive preferences). On the other hand cultural norms and societal structures to a large degree determine their individual capabilities. The capability approach thus allows taking these sources of inequality into account in the analysis.

Fernández-Baldor *et al.* (2014), recognizing this gender sensitivity of the capability approach, apply it in their evaluation of the above mentioned four energy projects in Peru, implemented by the regional office of Practical Action. According to this organization, which takes the household as the intervention and evaluation unit, the projects resulted in various livelihood and well-being improvements for the communities in question. The researchers confirm this, but in line with the capability approach they emphasize the multidimensional nature of well-being. As a consequence they broaden the informational base of their own evaluation, including dimensions not taken into account by Practical Action, 'such as spirituality, leisure, community participation, labour care, housework, and so forth' (p. 18). The perception of the researchers (p. 24) is that this broadening of the informational base, and the focus on the individual instead of the household, has enabled them to bring 'sensitive issues such as gender inequalities' up for discussion. The information collected reveals among others that the impact of the energy technology on the lives of men and women differs significantly. Having electric light at home in the evenings extends the leisure time for men, so Fernández-Baldor et al. find, while it extends the working time for women – who now have more time to finish household chores and do things to improve the welfare of their family members. Interestingly, however, women did not seem to mind spending more time on their family's welfare. The researchers briefly mention the notion of adaptive preferences, but do not discuss it in much detail. They thus leave open the probably controversial question of the implications of these findings for this type of project. Perhaps merely extending the informational base of project reports, as the researchers propose, would already be making some progress by raising awareness of gender-patterned consequences of new technologies.

Will the real capability approach stand up?

This chapter started out by presenting three broad and general perspectives on technology and poverty reduction, as discussed by Leach and Scoones – the 'race to the top', the 'race to the universal fix' and the 'slow race'. It was argued that the capability approach seems to be a natural ally of critics of the first two races, and of proponents of this 'slow race'. The AT movement was then discussed as an example of a more specific view on technology and poverty reduction fitting in with this 'slow race' perspective. On the one hand the capability approach seems to be very compatible with the AT movement, as both share an awareness of human diversity and – to some degree – value human agency. On the other hand the capability approach goes beyond the AT movement in the sense that it seems to be much more aware of and better able to deal with the value of agency and with gender issues. There are, however, at least two concerns which may be raised in response to this line of argumentation. The first is that the chapter so far insufficiently acknowledges that the capability approach is merely a conceptual framework and not a theory about empirical reality or phenomena in empirical reality – such as technology. It does not, for example, tell us much about the causes of poverty, or the factors which play a role in the successful implementation of a new technology. As pointed out in the Introduction, for most applications the capability approach needs to be supplemented with additional theories and accounts. However, what one sees through the lens of the capability approach may depend on which of such 'filters' one adds to it. The second concern, discussed in more detail below, is that the chapter so far has discussed 'the' capability approach, whereas in reality there exist many different versions. Only a limited number of normative or ethical claims, it has been argued by Robeyns (2014), are shared between all partisans of the approach. Both remarks come down to a concern that the chapter so far has been overestimating what the capability approach can do, and underestimating the degree to which people can still differ in opinion about matters even when they all adopt the capability approach as a key conceptual framework.

With respect to the second concern, it may be worth noting that between the two founders of the capability approach, Amartya Sen and Martha Nussbaum, differences exist in how they understand the capability approach (Crocker 2008; Robeyns 2005). For example, Sen is an economist by origin and his work takes social choice theory into account, whereas Nussbaum is a philosopher influenced by the work of Aristotle and adopts a much more narrative style. In addition there is now a massive literature on the capability approach from a range of other scholars, coming from different disciplines like economics, development studies, philosophy and many others. Not surprisingly, there are significant differences between publications in the way the capability approach is interpreted, applied and extended. Robeyns (2014) develops a 'concentric circle account' of the capability approach, based on the observation that only a very limited number of core normative commitments are shared by all capability scholars. In the outer circles of this concentric circles account one can then place specific versions of the capability approach, in which additional commitments are made. Central to the inner core circle is of course the claim that everybody should be able to lead a flourishing, truly human life – with functionings/capabilities as the main 'evaluative space' or 'informational base' for assessing this. A further claim, which was already discussed in the introduction, is that a normative evaluation of functionings/capabilities is needed. In addition, all versions of the capability approach acknowledge, according to Robeyns, that functionings/capabilities 'are not necessarily the only elements of ultimate value' (p. 13), and that there may be valid claims on what is right 'that do not refer to the capabilitarian notion of the good' (p. 14).[8] Finally, an essential feature of the capability approach is that it adopts a stance of ethical individualism (which will be further discussed in Chapter 3). In total, these claims are quite limited. They allow one to extend the capability approach for different purposes, such as for the assessment of quality of life (which is the focus of Sen), or for the development of a theory of justice (which is the focus of Nussbaum), or the conceptualization of a phenomenon like education or technology.

So what implications does this have for what was discussed in the previous sections? Let us start with the issue of agency. This concerns both the degree to which people are given an active role in technological development projects, and the ways in which such projects may – or may not – further increase people's ability to effectuate change in their community. Robeyns (2011) makes a distinction between a narrow and a broad usage of the capability approach in the literature. In its narrow application, she says, the capability approach is only concerned with the value of well-being, conceptualized in terms of individual functionings/capabilities. In its wider usage, the capability approach often takes a wider range of values into account, such as justice, efficiency, procedural fairness or agency.[9] Even Sen and Nussbaum have a difference of opinion on the topic of agency. Agency is, as we already saw, a concept or value that receives quite a lot of attention in the work of Sen. Nussbaum (2011: 200), however, finds the elaborate agency–well-being distinction as Sen makes it 'obscure and not useful'. She argues that 'all the important distinctions can be captured as aspects of the capability/ functioning distinction' (2000: 14), 'because what is valued is the freedom to do or not to do, agency is woven throughout' (Nussbaum 2011: 201). Nussbaum does assign an 'architectural role' to the capability of practical reason (number six on her list of ten), and this is 'probably a main site of agency in Nussbaum's approach' (Robeyns 2005: 105). Nussbaum thus seems to be more focused on agency as integral part of the *outcome* of a process of expanding people's capability set, whereas Sen pays more attention to the *process* of development itself and the role of agency in it.

Although not all capability scholars are thus on a par with respect to the exact meaning and role of agency, it is still undeniably true that agency is central in the work of many – although not all – capability scholars. This body of literature, and the ideas and insights discussed in it, can thus be of great value if one would like to argue for changes in current practices regarding technology and human development, just as Fernández-Baldor and colleagues do. Especially interesting is the agency-based development ethics of Crocker (2008), who takes the work of Sen as a point of departure. Among others he supplements it with insights from the literature on deliberative democracy, and work in development ethics on modes of participation. To make Sen's ideas about agency and development more tangible and concrete in relation to technology, one may also draw on a variety of existing studies in fields like science and technology studies (see e.g. Kullman and Lee 2012; Zheng and Stahl 2011) or design studies (see e.g. Frediani and Boano 2012; Nichols and Dong 2012). While all such publications on the capability approach and technology share some core commitments, they will inevitably also extend the approach in different ways.

Now let us also revisit the topic of gender. The capability approach may have several features that make it very suitable for addressing feminist concerns. One may nevertheless arrive at a different capability analysis or normative evaluation of certain gender cases, depending on whether one supplements the capability approach with a conservative/traditional or feminist theory explaining gender inequalities (Robeyns 2008). The example that she discusses in great detail is a fictive case of a Western couple. Both spouses received an education, but the woman leaves her job to become a full-time homemaker after having her first child. The conservative and the feminist would disagree on whether the woman and the man had an equal capability set to begin with, because they have a very different assessment of whether certain factors enable or constrain women and men – or to what degree. And they would disagree on whether the choice made by the woman to turn only certain capabilities into functionings is really a 'voluntary' or 'genuine' choice. The feminist would argue that there are problematic gendered constraints on the choices that women can make and/or that the preferences[10] underlying women's choices have been socially shaped in a morally problematic way. It seems, so Robeyns argues, that a feminist gender theory is a more natural supplement to the capability approach than a conservative one. Yet she warns that 'feminists should be concerned that the capability approach might be interpreted and applied in an androcentric way' (p. 101) – meaning that conscious or unconsciously there is a bias in favour of 'male' characteristics. A result of such bias could for example be that factors which limit women's capabilities are not acknowledged. Gender issues moreover raise difficult ethical questions regarding the best course of action, to which the capability approach alone does not give a simple and straightforward answer.

Let us get back to the AT projects which were discussed before. In the case of the energy projects in Peru, Fernández-Baldor et al. (2014) speculate that approaching the gender dimension 'from other more radical approaches' (p. 24) could have encountered opposition from local Practical Action staff. They thus chose not to combine the capability approach with such 'more radical' gender theories in their analysis and recommendations. In the case of the mp3 players in Zimbabwe, one possible solution – one in line with the idea of making technology 'appropriate' for the circumstances – would have been to anticipate the different conversion factors for women, and increase the maximum volume of the system so that also women seated 'second row' can hear the podcasts. In terms of the distinction of Molyneux (1985) between practical and strategic/transformative gender interests, this would have been a case of addressing the former – improving the situation of women within the status quo, without addressing structural injustice. Addressing strategic gender interests would mean instead addressing the root causes of an unfair status quo – such as unjust gender norms.[11] However, addressing structural injustice is often only possible through difficult transformation processes, which may fail. There is then a risk that the intended outcomes of the technological development project in question may not be realized. This is not just a dilemma for gender issues. More generally, it has been mentioned as one of the advantages of appropriate technology that 'it is less disruptive to the [existing] social structure' (Hazeltine and Bull 1999: 6), which increases the chances of a successful adoption of the new technology. The podcasting project of Practical Action as well was set up with the intention of not disrupting the social and political status quo in the community too much (Grimshaw and Gudza 2010), as will be discussed in more detail in Chapter 4.

The dilemma applies not only to the AT movement. Smith et al. (2014: 114) discuss it as one of the three challenges for all grass-roots innovation movements that one attempts 'being appropriate to existing situations that one ultimately seeks to transform'. There is therefore always a genuine question of which short-term and long-term development goal(s) to prioritize, and the capability approach as a general conceptual framework provides no simple algorithm to answer such questions. Yet capability analyses may play a useful role in such deliberations, as they do require assessing the magnitude and moral importance of existing (gender) inequalities.

Complementary views on technology and human development

Having discussed agency and gender, let us come back now to the three 'races' of Leach and Scoones (2006). The usage of the word 'race' to label these views on the relation between technology and poverty reduction – apart from the fact that the 'slow race' is clearly not a race at all – seems to have the rhetorical effect of discrediting the first two views.[12] Although Leach and Scoones indeed argue in their pamphlet that the 'slow race' deserves more attention, they do note that these three races are not mutually exclusive. They can even be seen as complementary strategies to reduce poverty. There is also nothing in the capability approach as a general conceptual framework that resists such view. In any domain of application it can generally be combined with a range of other accounts; it allows for a variety of additional normative commitments, as well as for different understandings of empirical reality. For example, Nussbaum (2006: 306–24) sees a central role for governments and (inter)national institutions in making sure that each and every person worldwide has all the capabilities on her list up to at least a certain threshold level. This may very well be a position that many capability scholars share. It is however not inconsistent to accept the core normative commitments of the capability approach 'while also believing a society in which all people have the capabilities needed to flourish is better reached by a coordinated commitment to individual action or by relying on market mechanisms' (Robeyns 2014: 27). Likewise, the capability approach may seem to have a natural fit with the 'slow race', due to a shared emphasis on human diversity and agency. However, it is certainly not a priori incompatible with the 'race to the top' or the 'race to the universal fix'. Indeed, the UNDP's Human Development paradigm has been profoundly influenced by Sen's work on the capability approach, but its 2001 report still promotes technological breakthroughs and technology-driven economic growth as important means to poverty reduction.

An insightful discussion of poverty reduction, innovation and economic development from the perspective of the capability approach can be found in a recent book by Hartmann (2014). It disentangles the complex and diverse ways in which innovation, structural economic change and human development are interrelated. The capability approach, Hartmann notes, challenges the idea that economic growth will automatically trickle down to the poor. 'However, proposing a bottom-up view from the individual's perspective', he fears, 'can lead to an equally problematic "trickle up" assumption: that the provision of basic capabilities [health, education, etc.] for individuals automatically leads to the structural features, institutions, incentives and scale effects required for innovation and structural change' (p. 64). And these are for several reasons essential to human well-being and agency. What the capability approach could contribute to innovation economics is a widening of the research perspective by providing a conceptualization of the ultimate goals of development (Cozzens *et al.* 2007). Rather than focusing on growth, stability or efficiency at a macroeconomic level, Hartmann (2014: 64) argues, we should look at economic meso-structures and aim to understand 'how the dynamics at a more disaggregated level affect people's choices and capabilities'. The question is not so much whether technology-driven economic growth can contribute to increasing human agency and well-being, but *which types* can do so and *how* these types could be promoted. It is for example important to acquire an understanding of how innovation capabilities and innovation systems can be fostered in the global South, which can lead to policies effectively stimulating economic growth. But it is even better to get an understanding of how to create virtuous cycles between economic growth, national innovation capacities and those individual human capabilities that empower people to lead the lives they have reason to value – or how to foster *inclusive* innovation systems which are responsive to social needs (Capriati 2013).

It should also not be left unmentioned that many different criticisms – of a technical, economic, physical, cultural, social and political nature – on the AT movement have been voiced over time (Willoughby 1990: ch. 9). One such criticism has been that implementing low-tech technologies will not stimulate the local development of technological skills or innovation capacities. The country in question will, according to this criticism, therefore not be enabled to move on to more sophisticated technologies over time (Hazeltine and Bull 1999: 277; Willoughby 1990: 237). Whether this criticism is valid or not is an empirical question that needs to be, and has been, addressed by innovation scholars. Discussing the evidence so far is beyond the scope of this book. Another example of a critique that has been voiced on the AT movement is that it 'died because it was led by well-intentioned tinkerers instead of hard-nosed entrepreneurs designing for the market' (Polak and Warwick 2013: 110). The capability approach as a normative conceptual framework, without additional 'explanatory theories' and relevant empirical data, does not have much to say about the truth or importance of most of such criticisms, nor about the desirability of alternatives for the AT movement. Take for example KickStart, a non-profit social enterprise operating in Africa. Through personal experiences its founders became greatly disappointed in the AT movement's lack of lasting impact on poverty reduction (Fisher 2006: 10). The capability approach warns us, among others, not to confuse means and ends. That does not seem to be a problem in this case. The article makes clear that the KickStart organization believes that technologies need to be 'designed to create individual opportunities', and that impact is ultimately about things such as enabling people to send their kids to school, or to improve their diet and health. But Fisher and his KickStart co-founders also believe (p. 10) that 'money is the primary means' towards achieving such goals, considering that people cannot avoid being or becoming part of a cash economy. And they believe that for this purpose it is best to put technology to work in a certain way. Thus KickStart 'focuses solely on technologies that are directly used to create income' and – contrary to the AT movement – puts central 'high-quality engineering and mass-production' (p. 20). KickStart claims that their technologies have enabled many thousands of people to run a profitable small-scale business, and improve their lives as a consequence. The capability approach does not deny that income is often an important means for the expansion of valuable capabilities, nor that entrepreneurship has a role to play in human development. Do such initiatives truly empower people – in all their human diversity – to lead the lives they have reason to value? That is, according to the capability approach, the key question.

Notes

1   A draft version of this chapter was presented at the 2014 HDCA conference, 2–5 September 2014 in Athens, Greece.
2   www.gatesfoundation.org/GlobalHealth/BreakthroughScience/GrandChallenges/Announcements/Announce-050627.htm (accessed by Leach and Scoones, 28 May 2006).
3   See Riley (2008: ch. 2) on engineering mindsets and stereotypes.
4   See e.g. Wyatt (2008).
5   A previous version of the remainder of this section appeared in Oosterlaken *et al.* (2012).
6   http://practicalaction.org/micro-hydro-power, accessed 21 March 2014. From the chapter by Fernández-Baldor *et al.* (2012) it does not become clear whether the cases discussed in their chapter are implemented by Practical Action or by another organization.
7   For an exploration of how the capability approach could more concretely be integrated in development management methodology, see Ferrero y de Loma-Osorio and Zepeda (2014).

8 How 'the right' and 'the good' relate is a difficult question that has been much debated among philosophers, but one that is beyond the scope of this book. Robeyns (2014, p. 14) gives the following example: 'consider the following claim: "choosing a dictatorship as the political regime for governing a country is always wrong". This claim concerns the right, which makes no reference to an account of value [the good]. A more specified capabilitarian theory could endorse this claim without making reference to [the good in terms of] people's functionings and capabilities to justify that claim.'
9 'Narrow' is thus not reflecting a value judgement. In the same paper Robeyns also discusses a different way of contrasting a narrow and wide usage of the capability approach, namely capability scholars who discuss the assessment of individual well-being (narrow usage), versus capability scholars who investigate the evaluation of policies and social institutions/practices contributing to or hampering well-being (wide usage).
10 Thus it also matters which theory of preference formation one combines with the capability approach.
11 Molyneux's distinction and its applicability to this case was kindly brought to my attention by Dorothea Kleine. The original publication on the case (Oosterlaken et al. 2012) insufficiently addresses the gender issue.
12 Moreover, those who emphasize the importance of growth and competitiveness may do so precisely because they believe it is *not* a zero-sum game – which a race by definition is. This point was kindly brought to my attention by Martin van Hees.

References

Capriati, M. (2013). Capabilities, Freedoms and Innovation: Exploring Connections, *Innovation and Development* 3(1):1–17.

Cozzens, S.E., Gatchair, S., Kim, K.-S., Ordóñez, G. and Supnithadnaporn, A. (2007). Knowledge and Development. In: Hackett, E.J., Amsterdamska, O., Lynch, M., and Wajcman, J. (eds), *The Handbook of Science and Technology Studies*. Cambridge, MA: MIT Press.

Crocker, D.A. (2008). *Ethics of Global Development: Agency, Capability, and Deliberative Democracy*. Cambridge: Cambridge University Press.

Crocker, D.A. and Robeyns, I. (2010). Capability and Agency. In: Morris, C.W. (ed), *Amartya Sen*. Cambridge: Cambridge University Press.

Fernández-Baldor, Á., Boni, A., Lillo, P. and Hueso, A. (2014). Are Technological Projects Reducing Social Inequalities and Improving People's Well-being? A Capability Approach Analysis of Renewable Energy-based Electrification Projects in Cajamarca, Peru. *Journal of Human Development and Capabilities* 15(1): 13–27.

Fernández-Baldor, Á., Hueso, A. and Boni, A. (2012). From Individuality to Collectivity: The Challenges for Technology-Oriented Development Projects. In: Oosterlaken, I. and Van den Hoven, J. (eds), *The Capability Approach, Technology and Design*. Dordrecht: Springer.

Ferrero y de Loma-Osorio, G. and Zepeda, C.S. (2014). Rethinking Development Management Methodology: Towards a Process Freedoms Approach. *Journal of Human Development and Capabilities* 15(1):28–46.

Fisher, M. (2006). Income Is Development: KickStart's Pumps Help Kenyan Farmers Transition to a Cash Economy. *Innovations: Technology, Governance, Globalization* 1(1):9–30.

Frediani, A.A. (2007). Participatory Methods and the Capability Approach. In: *Briefing Notes*. Human Development and Capability Association.

Frediani, A.A., and Boano, C. (2012). Processes for Just Products: The Capability Space of Participatory Design. In: Oosterlaken, I., and Van den Hoven, J. (eds), *The Capability Approach, Technology and Design*. Dordrecht: Springer.

Grimshaw, D.J. and Gudza, L.D. (2010). Local Voices Enhance Knowledge Uptake: Sharing Local Content in Local Voices. *Electronic Journal on Information Systems in Developing Countries (EJISDC)* 40(3):1–12.

Hartmann, D. (2014). *Economic Complexity and Human Development: How Economic Diversification and Social Networks Affect Human Agency and Welfare*. Routledge: New York.

Hazeltine, B. and Bull, C. (1999). *Appropriate Technology; Tools, Choices, and Implications*. San Diego/London: Academic Press.

Ibrahim, S. (2006). From Individual to Collective Capabilities: The Capability Approach as a Conceptual Framework for Self-Help. *Journal of Human Development* 7(3):397–416.

Juma, C., and Yee-Cheong, L. (2005). Innovation: Applying Knowledge to Development. In: UN Millennium Project, Task Force on Science, Technology, and Innovation. London: Earthscan.

Kullman, K., and Lee, N. (2012). Liberation from/Liberation within: Examining One Laptop per Child with Amartya Sen and Bruno Latour. In: Oosterlaken, I. and Van den Hoven, J. (eds), *The Capability Approach, Technology & Design*. Dordrecht: Springer.

Leach, M. and Scoones, I. (2006). *The Slow Race; Making Technology Work for the Poor*. London: Demos.

Lucena, J., Schneider, J. and Leydens, J.A. (2010). Making the Human Dimensions of Sustainable Community Development Visible to Engineers. *Engineering Sustainability* 164(ES1):13–23.

Mohan, G. (2008). Participatory Development. In: Desai, V. and Potter, R.B. (eds), *The Companion to Development Studies*. London: Hodder Education.

Molyneux, M. (1985). Mobilization without Emancipation? Women's Interest, the State and Revolution in Nicaragua. *Feminist Studies* 11(2):227–54.

Nichols, C. and Dong, A. (2012). Re-Conceptualizing Design through the Capability Approach. In: Oosterlaken, I. and Van den Hoven, J. (eds), *The Capability Approach, Technology & Design*. Dordrecht: Springer.

Nieusma, D. (2004). Alternative Design Scholarship: Working Towards Appropriate Design. *Design Issues* 20(3):13–24.

Nieusma, D. and Riley, D. (2010). Designs on Development: Engineering, Globalization, and Social Justice. *Engineering Studies* 2(1):29–59.

Nussbaum, M.C. (2000). *Women and Human Development: The Capability Approach*. New York: Cambridge University Press.

Nussbaum, M.C. (2006). *Frontiers of Justice: Disability, Nationality, Species Membership.* Cambridge, MA: Belknap Press of Harvard University Press.

Nussbaum, M.C. (2011). *Creating Capabilities: The Human Development Approach.* Cambridge, MA: Belknap Press of Harvard University Press.

Oosterlaken, I., Grimshaw, D.J. and Janssen, P. (2012). Marrying the Capability Approach, Appropriate Technology and STS: The Case of Podcasting Devices in Zimbabwe. In: Oosterlaken, I. and Van den Hoven, J. (eds), *The Capability Approach, Technology and Design.* Dordrecht: Springer, pp. 113–33.

Polak, P. and Warwick, M. (2013). *The Business Solution to Poverty: Designing Products and Services for Three Billion New Customers.* San Francisco, CA: Berrett-Koehler Publishers.

Riley, D. (2008). *Engineering and Social Justice.* San Rafael, CA: Morgan & Claypool.

Robeyns, I. (2005). The Capability Approach – A Theoretical Survey. *Journal of Human Development* 6(1):94–114.

Robeyns, I. (2008). Sen's Capability Approach and Feminist Concerns. In: Alkire, S., Comim, F. and Qizilbash, M. (eds), *The Capability Approach: Concepts, Measures, Applications.* Cambridge: Cambridge University Press, pp. 82–104.

Robeyns, I. (2011). The Capability Approach. In: Zalta, E. N. (ed.), *Stanford Encyclopedia of Philosophy.*

Robeyns, I. (2014). Capabilitarianism. Available at Social Science Research Network (SSRN), http://ssrn.com/abstract=2482007 (accessed 24 November 2014).

Roy, A. (1999). *The Cost of Living.* New York: Random House.

Schumacher, E. F. (1973). *Small Is Beautiful: A Study of Economics As If People Mattered.* London: Vintage.

Schuurman, F.J. (2008). The Impasse in Development Studies. In: Desai, V. and Potter, R. B. (eds), *The Companion to Development Studies.* London: Hodder Education.

Scott, A. and Foster, M. (2008). Gender, Technology and Livelihoods. In: Desai, V. and Potter, R. B. (eds), *The Companion to Development Studies.* London: Hodder Education.

Sen, A. (1984). *Resources, Values and Development.* Oxford: Blackwell.

Sen, A. (1985). *Commodities and Capabilities.* Amsterdam/New York: North-Holland.

Sen, A. (1992). *Inequality Reexamined.* Cambridge, MA: Harvard University Press.

Sen, A. (1995). Gender Inequality and Theories of Justice. In: Nussbaum, M. and Glover, J. (eds), *Women, Culture and Development: A Study of Human Capabilities.* Oxford, Clarendon Press, pp. 259–73.

Sen, A. (1999). *Development as Freedom.* New York: Anchor Books.

Shiva, V. (1991). *The Violence of the Green Revolution: Third World Agriculture, Ecology, and Politics.* London: Zed Books.

Shiva, V. (2001). The Seed and the Spinning Wheel – the UNDP as Biotech Salesman: Reflections on the Human Development Report – 2001. Available at www.iatp.org/documents/seed-and-the-spinning-wheel-the-undp-as-biotech.doc (accessed 10 April 2015).

Smith, A., Fressoli, M. and Thomas, H. (2014). Grassroots Innovation Movements: Challenges and Contributions. *Journal of Cleaner Production* 63(0):114–24.

Stamp, P. (1989). *Technology, Gender and Power in Africa.* Ottawa: International Development Research Centre.

Stewart, F. (2005). Groups and Capabilities. *Journal of Human Development* 6(2):185–204.
Suchman, L. (2008). Feminist STS and the Sciences of the Artificial. In: Hackett, E.J., Amsterdamska, O., Lynch, M. and Wajcman, J. (eds), *The Handbook of Science and Technology Studies*. Cambridge, MA: MIT Press.
Thirwall, A.P. (2008). Development and Economic Growth. In: Desai, V. and Potter, R.B. (eds), *The Companion to Development Studies*. London: Hodder Education.
UNDP. (2001). *Human Development Report 2001: Making New Technologies Work for Human Development*. New York: Oxford University Press.
Willoughby, K.W. (1990). *Technology Choice; A Critique of the Appropriate Technology Movement*. Boulder, CO/San Francisco, CA: Westview Press.
Willoughby, K.W. (2005). Technological Semantics and Technological Practice: Lessons from an Enigmatic Episode in Twentieth-Century Technology Studies. *Knowledge, Technology, & Policy* 17(3–4):11–43.
Wyatt, S. (2008). Technological Determinism Is Dead: Long Live Technological Determinism. In: Hacket, E.J., Amsterdamska, O., Lynch, M. and Wajcman, J. (eds), *The Handbook of Science and Technology Studies*. Cambridge, MA: MIT Press, pp. 165–80.
Zheng, Y. and Stahl, B.C. (2011). Technology, Capabilities and Critical Perspectives: What Can Critical Theory Contribute to Sen's Capability Approach? *Ethics and Information Technology* 13(2):6.

2
THE DETAILS OF TECHNOLOGICAL DESIGN

Technical artefacts, capabilities and the good life

The appropriate technology movement took an interest in engineering design – more particularly in the appropriateness of technical artefacts for their context of implementation. This chapter will further explore the topic of the design of technical artefacts from the perspective of the capability approach. It will do so from an understanding of the capability approach as a *normative* framework, in which well-being and agency are arguably the two key values – which both can, to an important extent, be understood in terms of valuable individual human capabilities. The second section will discuss well-being and design by making a connection between the capability approach and existing design approaches which pay attention to values. It introduces the idea of 'design for capabilities' or 'capability sensitive design'. The third section will address two challenges for such design, namely what Van de Poel (2012) has called the 'aggregation challenge' and the 'epistemological challenge'. The fourth section will explore several ways in which a connection can be made between the value of agency and design. The chapter will end with a reflection on the practical implementation of the ideas put forward in this chapter. However, before discussing any of this, this section[1] will first provide some background reflections on the role of technology in enabling people to lead a good life, a life they have reason to value. What will be argued is that technical artefacts could be seen as standing in a triangular relation to human capabilities and views of the good life (Figure 2.1, some examples will be mentioned in the next sections). Ideas of the good life create a need for technical artefacts, which expand the human capabilities that make it possible to realize such a view of the good life. Alternatively, one could say that ideas of the good life can be made concrete in terms of a set of required capabilities, which get created by means of technical artefacts.

Let us look at each of the three sides of this triangle in some more detail, starting with the relation between *views of the good life and human capabilities* (bottom arrow in Figure 2.1). 'Good' is not used here in the sense of morally right and wrong, the sense in which saints lead a good life and mass murderers a bad life. Rather, what we are interested in is what makes a life good – or worth living – for the person living that life. Unavoidably people will have very different, yet reasonable, particular ideas about what sort of life is a good life. The capability approach sees people as agents that try to shape their own life in light of such ideas. According to Sen (1985: 70) 'the "good life" is partly a life of genuine choice, and not one in which the person is forced into a particular life – however rich it might be in other respects'. Nussbaum (2000: 72) conceptualizes the human being as 'a dignified free being who shapes his or her own life', and elaborates that 'we see the person as having activity, goals, and projects' (p. 73). This general picture applies as much to people in the global North as to people in the global South – we are all human, after all. Not only is poverty – being one form of the absence of well-being – experienced as having many dimensions, the 'poor' also aspire to becoming more of an agent in their own lives (Narayan *et al.* 2000). A normative claim central to the capability approach is that each and every person should have the real and effective freedom – in other words the capabilities – needed to realize a life they have reason to value. Generally speaking, a flourishing human life will consist of a number of different components – well-being is considered to be multidimensional in the capability approach. People thus need capabilities in a range of different areas. The size and composition of a person's capability set will determine what sort of lives are within a person's reach. The concept of human capabilities is helpful in making the connection between broad and general views of the good life and concrete technical artefacts. 'Because the theory is essentially naturalistic and functionalist in orientation', Johnstone (2007: 84) claims, 'capability analyses are able to integrate descriptive and normative dimensions in a way that is particularly appropriate to technological domains'. She makes no extensive argument for this claim, but it could be understood as

48 The details of technological design

follows. Capabilities have a descriptive dimension in the sense that they are about the real, effective possibility of actual persons to do certain things and be in certain ways. The capability approach has a naturalistic orientation in the sense that whether a person has certain capabilities depends on the combination of natural and social forces at play, there is nothing 'supernatural' about capabilities. And as capabilities can be both means and ends and can be articulated at different levels of abstraction, it is in principle possible to reason about the relationships between various capabilities in a way that may appeal to engineers and designers. At the same time capabilities have a normative dimension according to the capability approach, in the sense that we recognize that some capabilities have an ethical value as constituents of a good life.

Let us also explore the other two sides of the triangle in some more detail. The connection *'good life–technical artefacts'* (upper-right arrow in Figure 2.1) is discussed, for example, by historian of technology Basalla (1989), who notes that an enormous diversity in technical artefacts worldwide has come into existence throughout history. He concludes from his research that it can be neither explained by bare human needs for which technology provides a solution, nor by varieties in climate and natural resources. Artefactual diversity has to be explained, Basalla claims (p. 217), 'as the material manifestation of the various ways men and women throughout history have chosen to define and pursue existence'. Basalla was, according to Van den Hoven (2012b), heavily influenced by the philosophical anthropology of Ortega Y Gasset (1972; 1961), who discusses the human condition and likewise argues that technology and the good life are intimately related. Ortega y Gasset (1961) argues that 'man's desire to live … is inseparable from his desire to live

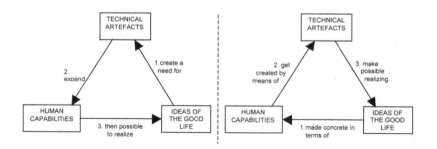

Figure 2.1 The basic triangle 'technical artefacts–human capabilities–the good life'

well',[2] which creates a need for technology, the development of which is given direction by ideas of the good life. Both religious conceptions of the good life and mundane life programmes, Van den Hoven (2012a: 331) asserts, 'come with technological assumptions, requirements and implications'. One example that he gives of such implications is that it is hard to imagine that intensive farming and weapons of mass destruction are being developed in a Buddhist community where becoming a Bodhisattva is commonly accepted as the best one could achieve in life – a Bodhisattva being somebody who is compassionately devoted to attaining enlightenment in order to relieve the suffering of all living beings. And an example of technological requirements that Van den Hoven gives is that 'the gentleman needs leisure, sports, lots of running water, a water closet, clean shaves, etc.'. In short, ideas about the good life are at least to a certain extent expressed in terms of our technical artefacts. What about the connection *'technical artefacts–human capabilities'* (upper-left arrow in Figure 2.1)? That there exists an intimate connection between human capabilities and technical artefacts could be established either by empirical research, or by engaging in philosophy of technology. In recent years several philosophers of technology have expressed, clarified and discussed in different ways the idea that all technical artefacts are by their very nature meant to expand human capabilities (Illies and Meijers 2014; Lawson 2010; Oosterlaken 2012; Van den Hoven 2012b).[3] The most directly expanded capabilities may of course be merely instrumentally valuable capabilities (e.g. a hammer and nails expanding someone's capability to join timber). A chain of means–ends reasoning is then needed to make the link with the ultimately valuable human capabilities that are of concern to the capability approach (in case of the hammer e.g. the capability to provide adequate shelter, which Nussbaum lists as a component of the capability to have bodily health).

As Johnstone (2012) notes, in the first instance it may seem that there is a simple, straightforward role for technology in the capability approach: technical artefacts are mere instruments which, by virtue of the function that they have, expand the human capabilities of their users. In other words, they empower people to realize the life they have reason to value. There are, however, various ways in which one could criticize such a simple, instrumental view. I will mention four complications, which are in various ways interrelated. First, in the capability approach the term 'functionings' refers to both the 'doings' and 'beings' of people. The latter may depend not only on the technical function that artefacts are able to fulfil, but also and perhaps more on their cultural and symbolic value. Van den Hoven (2012b: 33) for example notes that 'technology is not only important to achieve certain functionings, it may also be necessary to be a particular type of person who is the subject of those functionings ... one cannot be a young urban professional without a mobile phone and laptop computer'. And that is not only because of the way these technical artefacts can be *used*. Second, technical artefacts are not mere instruments for better implementing *existing* views of the good life. The examples of being a gentleman or young urban professional, Van den Hoven points out, indicate that certain views of the good life only arise once certain technologies exist. Or perhaps rather co-develop along with technological development. Third, at least a part of this influence of technology on views of the good life can be discussed in terms of how we interpret broad and general capabilities, such as Nussbaum's capability for affiliation – our ability to live well with and toward others. For example, one can question whether Facebook has merely an instrumental role in expanding this timeless capability, or whether it has changed our understanding of what it means to have this capability (Coeckelbergh 2011). Finally, as Johnstone (2012) discusses, it is often not merely a technical artefact that expands human capabilities, but an artefact in combination with certain social practices (such as house-building practices, or personal hygiene practices). Remember also the example in the Introduction of bicycles expanding the capabilities of people because of the way they are integrated in certain health care practices – like serving as an ambulance. The next chapter will explore the social embedding of technical artefacts in more detail, and try to drive the implications through a bit further. For now it will suffice to adjust the triangle by incorporating these insights (Figure 2.2). In comparison to Figure 2.1 it includes new social practices as an important factor which determines how technical artefacts influence human capabilities. It also acknowledges that technical artefacts are not mere instruments for the implementation of *existing, timeless* ideas of the good life. Rather, technological development may also influence our ideas of what a good life is and how we should understand the capabilities which enable people to lead a good life.

The previous discussion on technology and the good life raises the question how we may develop and design technical artefacts in such a way that they make the best possible contribution to expanding the capabilities people have reason to value. Studies from fields like science and technology studies (STS) and philosophy of technology (PoT) may give us insights into how the elements in Figure 2.2 play out in concrete cases, and this may in turn be used in the process of reflecting on the development and design of new technologies. Take – again – the bicycle example.[4] What the capability

The details of technological design **51**

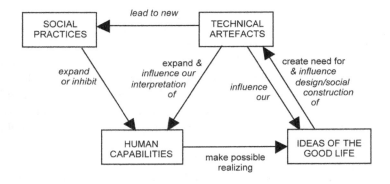

Figure 2.2 Adding social practices to the basic triangle

approach highlights is that ultimately 'we are not interested in a bicycle *because it is an object made from certain materials with a specific shape and colour*, but because it can take us to places where we want to go, and in a faster way than if we were walking' (Robeyns 2005: 98, emphasis added). Yet stopping there would be naïve regarding the insights gained in fields like design studies and STS. What we can learn from those fields is that if we indeed care about people's capability to lead a life they have reason to value, we should also – for instrumental reasons – care about the details of technological design. The colour of a technical artefact will in most cases probably not make much of a difference to people's capabilities, but its precise shape definitely will. A sociological/historical case study by STS scholar Bijker (1995) into the origins of the modern bicycle in Europe, covering a period of more than two centuries, illustrates this perfectly. Bijker's analysis shows that over time different social groups attached different meanings to this new artefact, and that this influenced its design. Initially, the bicycle was mainly viewed as a piece of sports equipment, used for racing contests. This means that achievable speed was very important. In the second half of the nineteenth century the high wheeled Ordinary bicycle had become the dominant model. It had a very large front wheel in comparison to the smaller rear wheel, and pedals connected directly to the front wheel. Because of the focus on speed, it developed in a direction of less rather than more safety (Bijker 1995: 43):

> The trend of enlarging the front wheel of the velocipede had continued once speed had become so important, and this made it necessary to move the saddle forward in order to keep pedals within

reach of the feet. This implied a reduction of the rear wheel's diameter – partly because otherwise the machine could not be mounted at all, partly to reduce the bicycle's weight, and partly for aesthetic reasons (it set off the grandeur of the high wheel). But these two developments moved the centre of gravity of the bicycle and rider far forward, to a position almost directly above the turning point of the system. Thus, only a very small counter force – for example, from the bumpiness of the road, but also from the sudden applications of the brake – would topple the whole thing.

Because of the bad condition of the roads in those days, this happened quite frequently. However, this was considered not as a problem, nor a sign of bad bicycle design. Cycling was considered to be an activity for young and adventurous men. The difficulty of riding the 'Ordinary' and its accident proneness, Bijker remarks, only contributed to the ability of these lads to impress the ladies, by participating in cycling contests in the parks. 'Falls were such an accepted part of bicycling', Bijker (p. 45) notes, 'that producers advertised their bicycles' ability to withstand falls, rather than claiming that they did not fall at all'. Thus, cycling was rarely undertaken by senior citizens or women, and certainly not considered as a form of transport. This, says Bijker, only changed 'when manufacturers began to regard women and older men as potential bicycle buyers'. The realization that there was a business opportunity here led to a whole series of new developments in bicycle design, with safety instead of speed now being a prominent goal. Some design changes were successful; others not. These attempts to reach new target groups led in the end to the dominance of the so-called 'safety bicycle', which is chain driven by the rear wheel. The main function of the bicycle was no longer sports; it had become transportion.

Of course one can always draw various lessons from such cases, depending on what one is interested in. Someone may want to highlight that bicycles which expand people's capability for transport were apparently not developed until somehow a business opportunity was perceived. However, one may also note that the details of bicycle design matter for which capabilities – recreation or transport – get expanded. And equally important is to note that ideas about the possible meaning of the bicycle for its users, about what it could allow them to do and be, was a factor shaping further technological development. It is not difficult to imagine that ideas about which capabilities enable people to lead flourishing, dignified human lives could be the inspiration for designing new and innovative technical artefacts.

Well-being and design[5]

The remainder of this chapter will further explore the topic of design from the perspective of the capability approach. This second section, and the next one, will focus on well-being as the central value in the capability approach. The fourth section will focus on agency as another key value in the capability approach literature. Naturally, capabilities will continue to play an important role in our conceptualization of the meaning of these values. With respect to design the focus of the remainder of this chapter will be on industrial design, although the occasional reference will also be made to other areas of engineering design, or to architectural design. The word 'design' has a double meaning: on the one hand as the *process* leading to designed products and artefacts; on the other, as the *outcome* of such a process. Both will to some degree be addressed. The chapter is also rather lenient towards what counts as 'design'. This could be conceptualizing and shaping a completely new artefact/system, redesigning and improving an existing artefact/system, or merely trying to figure out the best configuration of an artefact/system based on existing components and technologies. In the course of the chapter a link will be made between the capability approach and a number of roughly compatible design approaches. This can be seen as a way to 'operationalize' the capability approach in the area of design, but at the same time it will be investigated what added value the capability approach might have for these design approaches.

The idea of looking at design from the perspective of the values central in the capability approach fits in with developments in contemporary ethics of technology. One widely shared contemporary insight in this area of applied ethics is that technical artefacts are not merely value-neutral means towards human ends, but that they tend to be inherently normative (Radder 2009) or value laden (Van de Poel 2009).[6] Therefore not only human action, including how we use technology, is in need of ethical scrutiny – technology itself is as well. Moreover, technological design is not fixed by what is scientifically or rationally 'best'. Many different design options are generally available during the development process of a new technology or product, and these may or may not embed, respect or reflect moral values such as well-being, agency and many others. In other words: in this perspective the details of design are morally significant. The implication is that we should take values proactively into account during the design of new technologies and products. This idea has been most comprehensively explored in the body of literature on value sensitive design (VSD), an approach which aims to take a wide range of values – such as well-being, privacy, autonomy, accountability and sustainability – into account in each design process (Friedman and Kahn 2003; Nissenbaum 2005; Van den Hoven 2007). The VSD methodology developed by Friedman and her colleagues proposes that conceptual, technical and empirical investigations are being integrated in an iterative process. The conceptual phase concerns 'philosophically informed analyses of the central constructs and issues under investigation' (Friedman and Kahn 2003: 3). Key questions include which values are relevant, how they should be understood (e.g. what do we mean by well-being or distributive justice?), and which trade-offs between conflicting values are acceptable (e.g. is lowering safety levels acceptable for achieving sustainability?). The technical investigation looks into the question how certain technological features may either promote or obstruct the realization of the relevant values as identified in the conceptual investigations. Such investigations should lead to the proactive design of technologies which promote the relevant values. Empirical investigations, finally, complement conceptual and technical investigations. Examples are research into aspects of the context of implementation that codetermine to what degree values will in the end be realized, and stakeholder research into people's perception of relevant values and their proper conceptualization. There exist also various bodies of design literature that focus on specific values, such as those on design for sustainability, design for trust, privacy by design, universal/inclusive design and participatory design (Van den Hoven et al. 2014). The second part of this chapter will discuss, among others, participatory design in relation to the value of agency.

This section and the next will further explore the idea of 'capability sensitive design' (Oosterlaken 2009) or 'design for capabilities' (Oosterlaken 2014) as a way to expand people's quality of life or well-being. Is this really a new perspective compared to 'standard' design? The answer to this question depends of course on what one would consider to be standard design. According to Leydens et al. (2014: 2) the standard mode of design that still 'prevails in many engineering design courses' is 'design for technology'. Such design primarily focuses on criteria like functionality, reliability and costs and on meeting the design specifications as determined by the client. From the perspective of the capability approach one would want to see a more people-centred approach to design. Fortunately some fields of design, like industrial design engineering, are nowadays more focused on people. For example a whole range of design methods has been developed under the heading of 'human-centred design' (Steen 2011). These may be useful to ensure that a design really contributes to people's well-being. Unfortunately, however, Buchanan (2001: 37) observes:

> we often forget the full force and meaning of the phrase – and the first principle which it ['human-centred design'] expresses. This happens, for example, when we reduce our considerations of human-centred design to matters of sheer usability and when we speak merely of 'use-centred design'. It is true that usability plays an important role in human-centred design, but the principles that guide our work are not exhausted when we have finished our ergonomic, psychological, sociological, and anthropological studies of what fits the human body and mind.

In other words: this approach still has the tendency to adopt a rather limited perspective on people and the purpose of design. Industrial designers are often mainly interested in creating products that evoke positive subjective user experiences, or on satisfying the preferences and desires of customers (Van de Poel 2012). Terms like comfort, pleasure, excitement, satisfaction, inspiration, happiness and other terms describing people's subjective experiences or mental states are common to the vocabulary of these designers (Oosterlaken 2009). It is not wrong to take these into account, it is even useful, but it should also be noted that there are various problems with relying exclusively on such subjective accounts of well-being. A focus on for example pleasure does not necessarily lead to design solutions that contribute to a person's long-term well-being. Another problem with subjective accounts of well-being is that of adaptive preferences – to which we will return later on in this chapter. In response to such problems philosophers have proposed various more objective accounts of well-being, for example based on what people would choose if they were well informed, or grounded in an account of human nature. Nussbaum's list of ten central categories of human capabilities is an example of a so-called 'objective list account' of well-being. Such accounts list the elements of well-being that should arguably be within everybody's reach, whether they desire them or not. Nussbaum's list may be a source of inspiration for designers and could be a starting point for a deeper conversation with users and stakeholders about what would truly contribute to people's well-being. In other words: the capability approach may serve as a reminder of the ultimate goal of design – improving people's well-being. More importantly, the capability approach provides a convincing, versatile and useful perspective on how well-being could be conceptualized and understood for the purposes of design – namely in terms of valuable human capabilities, what people are effectively able to do and be. It invites designers and engineers to look beyond what people superficially seem to want or prefer.

One advantage of thinking about well-being in terms of human capabilities is that this concept draws the designer's attention to relevant personal, social and environmental 'conversion factors'. These should be taken into consideration if one wants to make sure that some artefact or product (merely a means) can truly contribute to the expansion of valuable human capabilities (its ultimate end). If possible, one should already anticipate these factors during the design process and choose design features in response to these factors. It could be argued that it is part of the very nature of engineering design that conversion factors are proactively taken into account during good design – or at least to the degree necessary to deliver a functional artefact meeting the design requirements (Oosterlaken 2012). However, from the perspective of the capability approach one would like engineers to take into account a broader range of personal and structural factors. Of course plenty of designers already do this. The previous chapter argued that the appropriate technology movement was, without using the conceptual framework of the capability approach, very aware of relevant social and environmental factors more broadly. And no engineer would come up with a regular bicycle if (s)he was asked to design a means of transportation that should also be usable by people with paralysed legs. Still, with respect to personal differences between people, it has been noticed that designers often unconsciously assume that users are 'just like them' (Keates 2014). In response to that problem the universal/inclusive design movement arose, which is all about 'accounting for diversity' (Nieusma 2004: 14). One could say that just as the appropriate technology movement took social and environmental conversion factors into account, the universal design movement is taking personal conversion factors into account (Oosterlaken 2012). This movement assumes, say Connell and Sanford (1999: 49), 'that it is possible to design objects and spaces such that they are usable (and will be used) by a broad range of the population, including but not limited to people with disabilities'. There is often an ethical case to be made for making design more inclusive. A paradigm case is that of the demand that buildings are designed in such a way that they are also accessible by people in a wheelchair. Such inclusive architectural designs may greatly contribute to the goal of getting each and every person up to at least a certain threshold level of the capabilities needed to lead a flourishing life. Therefore Nussbaum (2006: 167) forcefully defends it as a basic requirement of justice. Arguably the inclusive/universal design has come up with solutions for some of the challenges of human diversity, thus contributing to the realization of the normative ideal of the capability approach that each and every person should have the capabilities to lead a life (s)he has reason to value. Yet taking a capability approach may still have some added value by (a) providing a vantage point from which to identify possibly relevant factors – starting from intrinsically valuable human capabilities as the goal may broaden the range of factors identified, and (b) prioritize them according to importance – namely in terms of the strength of their relationship to the capabilities that the design project aims to contribute to. Furthermore, the capability approach could play a role in the evaluation of design proposals. The capability approach makes it possible to make a quite natural connection between on the one hand movements such as those dealing with inclusive/universal design or appropriate technology, and on the other hand wider normative debates about justice and human well-being.

A positive feature of the capability approach is furthermore that it draws attention to the multidimensionality of well-being and to the possible interconnection between different capabilities. Often a technical artefact may most obviously contribute to a certain aspect of a person's well-being, related to the artefact's function. For example, when designing a malaria diagnostic device for use in rural areas in India (Kandachar *et al.* 2011), one obviously aims to contribute to people's capability to be healthy. On further reflection, however, technologies may have an impact on multiple capabilities, either directly or indirectly. Take for example the Chula, a cooking stove developed by Philips and sold in Indian villages. Using the capability approach to evaluate its impact, Mink *et al.* (2014) found that this technology is connected to people's capabilities to be well nourished, to be healthy, as well as people's capability to spend leisure time (which is connected to Nussbaum's capability for 'play'). It enabled them to prepare new types of food, and through its effect on smoke in the house it influenced their capability to be healthy. The impact on people's capability to spend leisure time was mixed; on the one hand the process of cooking became quicker, on the other hand more firewood was needed to be collected. According to Otte (2014) the use of firewood for cooking in many developing countries is known to lead to local deforestation, and such sustainability problems will also start to influence people's capability to earn a living. The time that girls have to spend on collecting firewood may also seriously diminish their capability to get an education. Solar cookers may be a solution, and according to Otte (p. 15) 'different cooking needs and habit' have led to the development of different types of cookers around the world. A mismatch between the solar cooker and existing social practices may, however, negatively influence its successful implementation and therefore the impact of the artefact on capability expansion. This occurs for example, Otte notices, when the solar cooker requires cooking outside, whereas the existing cultural practice is to cook inside. A change in the design could potentially solve this mismatch. None of the insights mentioned in the cooking stove example automatically follow from the capability approach as a broad and general conceptual framework, and neither is the capability approach necessary for discovering the relevance of any of the aspects mentioned. What this example does show is that making technology contribute to human development generally requires a 'comprehensive and holistic approach' of people's life, and this is exactly what the capability approach can offer (Robeyns 2011: 9) to designers.

In short, the perspective that the capability approach offers invites engineers and designers to look at a range of different dimensions of well-being, as well as to gain a deeper understanding of the people involved and the full context of implementation. This may not only lead to a different design for the technical artefact, product or system that the engineer or designer set out to create. It may also, Leydens *et al.* (2014) argue, lead to reframing or broadening the original design problem. An example of a project where an extensive analysis of the context and users led to a broad interpretation of the design problem can be found in a report by Bazoli (2011). She looked into the severe restrictions that women in rural India face when they are menstruating. Due to cultural taboos they have to avoid many of their usual day-to-day activities during this period, such as cooking and participating in religious practices. In order to solve this problem Bazoli designed a sanitary napkin that met local needs and was appropriate to the local context – paying attention to its full life cycle. In addition, she also designed an educative group game that addresses a related problem, namely the lack of knowledge that women have about menstruation symptoms.

The epistemological and aggregation challenge

The 'design for capabilities' approach argued for in the previous section does, however, raise challenges. Van de Poel (2012, forthcoming) identifies two key challenges for design for well-being more broadly, namely an epistemological and an aggregation challenge. He briefly discusses Nussbaum's capability list as one possible interpretation of well-being that can be of use to designers, yet this section presents a more in-depth discussion of these challenges from the perspective of the capability approach. Van de Poel (forthcoming) describes the epistemological or knowledge challenge for 'design for well-being' in general as follows:

> design typically concerns products that do not yet exist; in fact design is largely an open-ended process which relates to creating a product. This means that the designers not only need knowledge of [a] what constitutes well-being for users and how that well-being might be affected by new technologies, but they must also [b] be aware that such knowledge needs to be translated into, for example, design requirements, criteria or technical parameters that can guide the design process.

Let's start with sub-challenge [a]. This challenge can be expected to be extra salient in many 'design for development' or 'humanitarian engineering' projects, where often Western designers and engineers have to contribute to the well-being of people in a culture and context that they hardly know. Can the capability approach provide help here? Sen leaves it rather open which capabilities constitute well-being, while Nussbaum's version of the capability approach provides more guidance. However, a feature of Nussbaum's list of ten intrinsically valuable categories of capabilities is its 'multiple realizability' (Nussbaum 2000: 105). It still needs to be investigated what these rather abstract capabilities, such as the capability for play or affiliation, could mean exactly in the context or culture for which the design is meant. Moreover, the effect of new technologies on human capabilities, so the introductory chapter already argued, is dynamic and complex. They do not only depend on the design itself, but also on how the technology is embedded in its socio-technical context (as will be discussed in more detail in the next chapter). Designers need to be aware that this is the case and try to gain an understanding both of the relevance and meaning of certain capabilities and of the context of implementation for their design. Design for capabilities thus requires, as Van de Poel (2012: 301) remarks for design for well-being in general, 'more than just the identification of user demands by means of surveys or marketing research'. It requires – in the terminology of the Value Sensitive Design approach – extensive and integrated conceptual, technical and empirical investigations. Of course for both practical and epistemic reasons it is not realistic to expect designers to anticipate and take into account all possible capability impacts of their design. The work of designers will at a certain point need to become focused on the capabilities, conversion factors and issues that seem most salient and relevant to the design challenge in question.

An obvious and often defensible curtailment of the design scope, claims Van de Poel (2012: 295), will be to concentrate on the well-being of the expected direct users of a technology. One can wonder, he notes, whether designers have any moral obligation to also aim to increase the well-being of more indirect stakeholders. In contrast, ethicists mostly agree that the moral imperative not to harm other stakeholders cannot be dismissed that easily, which may sometimes mean that attention needs to be paid to the capability impacts for non-users. Take an example provided by Murphy and Gardoni (2012): infrastructural works such as bridges and dikes may also come with risks for non-users, which may be conceptualized as diminishing the security of their capabilities. There are strong ethical reasons for designers to take at least such harms into account as well. Moreover, in the context of 'design for development' or 'humanitarian engineering' it is often not individual users but communities which are the natural unit of concern and focus (Leydens et al. 2014). This means that it is not possible to reduce the epistemological challenge by focusing on a homogeneous group of people.

In another article Van de Poel (2013) has reflected on sub-challenge [b], translating values into design requirements, criteria and so on. It has also been proposed that VSD always includes the activities of the discovery, translation and verification of values (Flanagan et al. 2008). The translation process, Van de Poel (p. 256) warns, 'may be long-lasting and cumbersome', it 'may require specific expertise, sometimes from outside engineering', it 'is value laden', 'can be done in different ways' and is 'context-dependent'. That last point may be considered to be especially important from the perspective of the capability approach, considering its emphasis on human diversity and the great variety of personal, social and environmental conversion factors. A central idea in Van de Poel's paper on how to translate values into design requirements is that of a 'value hierarchy' going from (a) abstract values, via (b) norms to (c) concrete design requirements – where each of these three main layers may have sub-layers again. An example that he gives is that of animal welfare as a central value in the design of chicken husbandry systems. This value may be translated into norms such as 'presence of laying nests', 'enough living space' and so on. The latter norm could in turn be translated in a requirement such as having at least a 1,100 cm^2 usable area per hen. Constructing such a value hierarchy may also be useful for design for well-being. According to Van de Poel (p. 265) the exercise of creating such a value hierarchy serves two purposes. First, it makes the process of translating values into design requirements more systematic. Second, 'it makes the value judgments involved also explicit, debatable and transparent'. This already seems very helpful, even though – as Van de Poel notices – merely describing a value hierarchy does not directly solve possible disagreements about such translations.

Van de Poel does not further specify sub-layers for the three layers that he mentions. However, with respect to the level of values it makes sense to keep in mind a distinction, among others made by Rawls (1999: 5), between the concept of a value and the conception of a value. The concept is the general idea of a value, such as well-being, justice or sustainability. The conception is a specific interpretation or understanding of the exact meaning of that value. For example, very few people will deny that well-being is an important value. However, as we saw, there are very different ways in which one can understand this value. One could adopt a subjective conception of well-being, for example the conception that well-being consists of the satisfaction of whatever desires people may have. Or one could adopt an objective conception of well-being, according to which well-being consists of people having certain universally valuable elements from a list – for example Nussbaum's list of ten central categories of capabilities. While constructing a value hierarchy it is important to make explicit which conception of a value one adopts, as depending on this choice one may arrive at different norms and subsequently at different design requirements. If one adopts the capability approach as one's conception of well-being, the next question to ask would be which capabilities are relevant to the case at hand. As Nussbaum's list of capabilities is deliberately quite general and abstract, further specification will be needed. One way to further specify the capabilities on her list is to formulate context-dependent interpretations. Another way to further specify the capabilities on her list is to define more concrete capabilities which are important for the sake of the high-level capability. 'For the sake of', Van de Poel (p. 260) explains, is a general term that covers a range of more specific relations. A certain capability could, for example, be either a constitutive part of a higher-level capability, or be a means towards that capability. For example, one's capability to be free of malaria could be said to be constitutive of one's capability for bodily health – to which designers may for example contribute by creating a new malaria diagnostic device that is suitable for usage in rural areas in developing countries. As we have seen, many conversion factors may stand in the way of such a device leading to the expansion of the capability in question for, say, villagers in India. These factors can be an important source for norms and subsequent concrete design requirements – for example, the fact that local health care workers have little education may lead to a norm that the device should have a simple and intuitively clear user interface – a norm which then needs to be further translated into concrete design requirements.

In addition to the epistemological challenge, Van de Poel (2012: 296) notices that design for well-being will run into an aggregation problem, which

> arises due to the fact that a design does not affect the well-being of just one person, but rather that of a range of people. This raises the question of how the well-being of these people should be aggregated so that it can be taken into account in the design process. If one believes that well-being constitutes plural and incommensurable prudential values, as some philosophers … have suggested, then an aggregation problem arises with respect to how these values can, or cannot, be aggregated into an overall measure of well-being.

The capability approach indeed also faces both these problems of aggregation over (a) a range of people while not losing sight of the moral worth of each and every individual and (b) plural, incommensurable capabilities (Comim 2008). According to the capability approach well-being is multidimensional, as leading a flourishing human live entails the realization of 'beings and doings' in a range of different domains. People therefore always need a range of different capabilities, which are incommensurable; a high level of the capability to be healthy can, for example, not compensate for a low level of the capability of affiliation with other people. The incommensurability of values, Van de Poel (forthcoming) notes, 'limits the applicability of [maximizing] methods such as cost benefit analysis and multi-criteria analysis which are often used in technical design to choose between different conceptual design solutions'. These methods, after all, try to subsume very different considerations under one score. Luckily, he says, there exist alternative methods. He distinguishes between two different situations. The first is where design is supposed to contribute to elementary capabilities in contexts of great poverty. Here the solution that Van de Poel proposes is – in line with Nussbaum's position[7] – to 'set thresholds for all the relevant capabilities and to look for a design that reaches all of these thresholds'. The second situation is contexts where people enjoy greater levels of well-being. Here the focus will be on more intricate and complex capabilities rather than basic capabilities needed for survival, and one aims to find a design that contributes to the overall well-being of users. The solution that Van de Poel (2012) proposes consists of several elements. A basic step is to 'select a user group that shares a comprehensive [life] goal and/or a vision of the good life', which 'avoids the need to aggregate the well-being of people who have different, incompatible' (p. 303) goals or visions. The idea is then to define a mix of specific values (or capabilities, in the context of this chapter) and then to design a product or technology that makes the best possible contribution to realizing this mix. Van de Poel (p. 303) hastens to add here that this

> does not imply a maximising approach to well-being. The focus is on the mix of values [or capabilities] rather than on maximising an overall measure of well-being. The focus is also not on maximising each of the prudential values [or capabilities] in isolation, because it is usually the mix of values [or capabilities] that contributes to the overall goal rather than the values [or capabilities] in isolation.

Incommensurability of capabilities thus need not become a problem if creative design solutions enable us to expand all of them rather than to make a trade-off between them.

Van de Poel's idea of focusing on a mix of capabilities rather than on single ones shows some resemblance to the idea of a 'capability innovation', introduced by Ziegler (2010). He builds on Schumpeterian economics, which views development as a process of economic innovation in the sense that new combinations arise – new goods, methods of production and so on. Ziegler then defines social innovation as 'the carrying out of new combinations of capabilities' (p. 265). Using the insight that capabilities can be both ends in itself and means towards other capabilities, Ziegler explains that his concept of capability innovation highlights such relations. Of course new products and their design details may be an essential element in the success of such 'capability innovations'. A case that can illustrate this is that of the introduction of public toilets in Kenya by an organization called Ecotact (Ziegler *et al.* 2013). The project 'improves capabilities in the domain of health, bodily integrity and the social bases of respect for users', Ziegler *et al.* (p. 7) claim. 'On the other hand, it links this service to economic capabilities, creating jobs based on a public–private business model'. Design was an important factor in its success, as the buildings were designed as 'toilet monuments', as a consequence of which 'public sanitation is ... transformed from a matter of cultural taboo and humiliation to a widely recognized and talked about feature of urban centres'.

A project on tricycles for disabled people in Ghana, executed by industrial design engineering students (Kandachar et al. 2007, see also the discussion in Oosterlaken 2009) may also be taken to illustrate the idea of 'capability innovations'. Both the local context and entrepreneurial opportunities were carefully taken into consideration. During exploratory field studies it was discovered that 'the major part of the disabled population is willing to work but cannot find employment' and that 'the Ghanaian society is annoyed by disabled who are begging on the street' (p. 69). The newly designed tricycle has a cooler in front so that disabled users are able to make a living as street vendors selling ice-cream and other frozen products. It can be considered a capability innovation in Ziegler's sense, as it involves a new combination of simultaneously expanding for the capabilities for mobility, earning a living (and hence basic capabilities related to survival and health), social participation and self-esteem for people with certain disabilities.[8]

Agency and design

Having discussed a 'narrow' or well-being usage of the capability approach for design in some detail, I would now like to move to a 'broad' usage of the capability approach in the context of design. In a broader usage the capability approach is not only seen as highlighting the importance of individual well-being and conceptualizing this in terms of human capabilities, but is also seen as taking aboard a wider range of values, most importantly agency. The importance of agency in the capability approach is, as was already argued, among others reflected in the approach's defence of capabilities instead of functionings as a policy goal. The idea behind making a distinction between capabilities and functionings is to be respectful of people's agency and their views on the good life by focusing on expanding their capabilities without forcing them to realize the corresponding functionings.

In the case of the design of technical artefacts, one may wonder if it is sensible to uphold this capability–functioning distinction. Is an artefact which does not lead to the anticipated increase in functioning(s) a failure? The answer to this question is context dependent. If those people lacking the functioning have freely chosen not to realize it, those people are exercising their agency. We generally need to accept and respect this. As long as some people choose to realize the functioning(s) made possible by the technology, it apparently made some valuable contribution to people's life (although a lack of large-scale usage may be a problem from the commercial perspective in which many design projects take place). Moreover, in the view of the capability approach merely increasing people's freedom to achieve certain valuable beings and doings is already making a contribution to people's wellbeing. Yet if the functioning(s) in question are absent on a massive scale, this certainly warrants further investigation. Has the designer failed to grasp what functioning(s) could be important to people's lives? Or are there perhaps disruptive conversion factors in play that nobody foresaw and has the design therefore not really enabled people to realize these functioning(s)? This would mean that the design has not really led to empowerment or an increase of agency. These two causes, which can be distinguished when looking through the lens of the capability approach, obviously ask for different responses.

The capability–functioning distinction may also make designers aware of how much choice they are giving users (Kleine *et al.* 2012). The relation between technology and choice has been discussed by a number of philosophers of technology. Verbeek (2008: 95), for example, argues that all technical artefacts are active in the sense that 'they help to shape human actions, interpretations, and decisions, which would have been different without the artefact'. However, in the last decade there has been growing interest in the persuasive or behaviour-steering potential of technical design. Engineers/designers increasingly make a deliberate attempt to get people to act in certain ways – using among others insights from behavioural psychology. Examples can among others be found in the area of sustainable design (e.g. Lockton *et al.* 2008) and especially in ICT applications (e.g. Fogg 2003). This phenomenon may be more widespread and pervasive for the emerging/converging technologies that dominate debates in the global North, than for the 'appropriate' technologies introduced in many technological development projects. Yet even more 'low-tech' development or poverty reduction interventions can be intentionally persuasive. For example, Parmar *et al.* (2008: 104) describe a specific 'personal health information system' designed by them for 'motivating [Indian] rural women to challenge existing social beliefs and practices, thereby persuading them to follow correct health practices'.

Let us take a simple example, that of speed bumps, which are deliberately designed to cause car drivers to slow down. In terms of the capability approach, we can say that whereas before the driver had the capability to both speed and drive slowly, he is now forced into a certain functioning. Just as well, one could point out that for other traffic participants the speed bumps actually increase the capability to move around safely. It seems therefore easily justifiable from the perspective of the capability approach, as arguably the capability to move around safely seems to carry more moral weight than the capability to speed. Moreover, this is a case of drivers causing harm to other people. More controversial is the example of seatbelts. The presence of a seatbelt in a car merely increases the driver's *own* capability to be safe in traffic, cars with annoying sounds when you do not put on your seatbelt encourage the realization of the corresponding functioning, and cars that won't start until the driver fastens the seatbelt actually force her/him into this functioning. What the latter example illustrates is that technical artefacts may – because of their design features – sometimes do more than *merely* expanding a certain capability and leaving the choice to realize the corresponding functioning to the empowered user.

One might be inclined to think that such design practices and technologies are morally problematic from the perspective of the capability approach, as they seem to respect insufficiently people's agency. That is not so self-evident though. One reason is that different capabilities are often related in complex ways, with capabilities for example being valuable in themselves, as well as a means for other capabilities. Nussbaum (2000: 91) has argued that 'we may feel that some of the capabilities [like that of being healthy] are so important, so crucial to the development or maintenance of all others, that we are sometimes justified in promoting functioning rather than simply capability, within limits set by an appropriate concern for liberty'.[9] The personal health information system developed by Parmar *et al.* (2008) may very well fall within those limits. The question then becomes, of course, which limits arise from 'an appropriate concern for liberty', or how they can be determined. On the topic of seatbelt and helmet laws Nussbaum (p. 93) says that they 'reflect a wide-spread view that it is appropriate to protect people's long-term capabilities against the consequences of momentary carelessness'. Still, mechanical enforcement seems a step further than legal enforcement, and may fall outside of those limits. Many people will consider this seatbelt technology a trivial and unimportant infringement on their freedom to lead the lives they have reason to value, but one might reasonably challenge this.[10]

There is a further reason why it is not so clear-cut that persuasive or behaviour-steering technologies are incompatible with the capability approach. Although it is able to take into account 'the influence of societal structures and constraints on those choices' made by people (Robeyns, 2005: 108), 'the capability approach *as such* contains no normative theory of choice'

(Robeyns 2000: 19). Depending on which theory one selects, one may find certain persuasive or behaviour-steering technologies a problematic infringement on people's freedom to make their own choices in life, and others not. One of the major factors influencing people's choice is of course the preferences they have formed during the course of their life. In the Introduction it was explained that the capability approach focuses on capabilities rather than preference satisfaction as the main 'informational space' in which to assess well-being. This is among others because of the problem of so-called 'adaptive preferences' – preferences which are problematic due to them having been formed under conditions of extreme deprivation or oppression. The concept of adaptive preferences implies that respect for people's agency should not be taken to mean that designers always need to respect each and every preference that people happen to have. And persuasive or behaviour-steering technology may possibly even provide a solution to the problem. However, too easily labelling someone's preferences as 'adaptive' would lead to unjustified paternalism – which especially in the intercultural context of 'design for development' may quickly become an issue. Again, the capability approach *as such* does not contain a specific normative theory of preference formation that allows one to distinguish between problematic and unproblematic preferences (Robeyns 2000) – and as a consequence capability scholars may come to very different assessments, depending on how they supplement the capability approach. In addition, the capability approach also does not contain any knowledge on the different mechanisms that are at a designer's disposal to steer human behaviour. It would not be very useful to lump all such mechanisms together, instead of making relevant distinctions between them (e.g. between a mere noise when a seatbelt is not worn, and an impossibility to start the car). Certainly any normative theory of choice adopted would need to be used to investigate each of these mechanisms separately, rather than being used to immediately condemn persuasive or behaviour-steering technology overall. It will however remain hard if not impossible to provide general guidelines on how to balance the different concerns outlined in this section, abstracted from the details of concrete cases.

In short, the capability approach does not offer quick-and-easy guidelines for designers, but rather a conceptual framework that may make a small but valuable contribution to the ongoing debate on the ethics of persuasive and behaviour-steering technical design (e.g. Berdichevsky and Neuenschwander 1999; Davis 2009). Aspects that ethicists of technology identify as being important include the degree to which the user is made aware of the intentions of the designers (Atkinson 2006), the possibility to override preprogrammed choices, and whether it concerns 'more overarching goals or activities' rather than low-level ones (Brey 2006: 361). The latter may for example be done within an ethical evaluation of the value of different capabilities. In addition, the capability–functioning distinction may remain helpful, even though it is not simply the case that we should always merely promote capabilities and never force anyone into a functioning (Robeyns 2005). Figure 2.3 elaborates on Figures 2.1 and 2.2, taking into account what was discussed so far in this section.

The outcome or result of a new technology may be that people's agency is strengthened because of an increase in their capability set. However, an outcome may also be that their capability set or agency is decreased. Many capability theorists, first and foremost Amartya Sen, are however not only concerned with the outcomes of processes of development or social change, but also with the processes themselves. And one aspect of this concern is that people are not only 'patients' to be helped, but should be taken seriously as agents in the process leading to the outcome. This issue was extensively discussed in the Introduction and Chapter 1, which discussed the issue of participation in technological development projects. A connection can also be made with participatory design. According to Nieusma (2004: 16) participatory design should be all about dealing with different, conflicting views that users and stakeholders have. Over time a range of methods has been developed to involve people in the design process. He regrets, however, that 'increasingly, participatory design methodologies are used to advance the goals of user-centred design without emphasizing the inclusion of

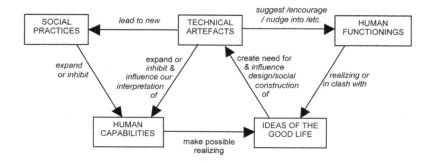

Figure 2.3 Extending the triangle with persuasive or behaviour-steering technology

The details of technological design **69**

marginalized perspectives in design processes' (p. 17). In other words: despite using participatory methods during the design process, people of marginalized groups are not really taken seriously as agents with views that deserve serious consideration. The capability approach may be helpful in revitalizing the ideals of participatory design (Oosterlaken 2009), for the same reasons that the capability approach may have added value for participatory methods in development cooperation more broadly (see Chapter 1). Frediani and Boano (2012: 205), who focus on urban design in the global South, note 'a surprising lack of literature investigating the conceptual underpinnings of participatory design and its implications in terms of practice', a gap which – according to them – could be filled with the help of the capability approach.

Going a step beyond 'mere' participation in a process where professional designers are still in the lead is proposed by Dong (2008), who uses the capability approach to make a connection between design practice and attempts to realize social justice. His focus is on the design of civic works and the built environment. He argues that such design is intimately connected to people's health and identity. Therefore Dong (p. 82) proposes to add 'control over the design and production of civic building' to Nussbaum's description of the tenth and final capability on her list of ten central human capabilities. It concerns the capability to have some 'control over one's environment', and Nussbaum divides it into two types of environments: the political and the material environment. The latter is unfortunately interpreted rather narrowly, as Nussbaum in her description of the capability to have control over one's material environment only talks about property, employment and being free from unwarranted search and seizure. It seems that one could easily extend Dong's argument to the design of technical artefacts more broadly; technologies are nowadays ubiquitous in all domains of human life. Considering insights on the 'politics' (Winner 1980) and 'value-ladenness' (Radder 2009) of such artefacts, it makes sense to also include the capability to have at least some control – however limited – over one's technological environment. But back to Dong's (2008: 77) line of argument:

> Public policies can effectively remove public engagement in the name of expediency … Thus, what the urban poor in developing countries and citizens in developed countries share is the problem of enacting a policy of design that reflects the values of the people … People have the right to user participation in design only if there are effective policies to make people truly capable of design. So what is needed is not user participation in design as a counterforce to the power of

designers ... but instead a design culture of pluralism with effective means for achieving it.

Dong argues that from a justice perspective we should pay attention to citizens' capabilities to design themselves and in this way enable them to co-shape their life world. For this purpose he fleshes out a set of instrumentally important capabilities that citizens would need to do design, which could become object of (inter)national design policy. The categories that he distinguishes are information, knowledge, abstraction, evaluation, participation and authority. Dong points out, in line with the capability approach, that 'asymmetries in capability to do design may arise from differences between people and socio-political barriers' (p. 83). Design policy should thus address both these internal and external factors. As Nichols and Dong (2012) explicate: gaining design capacity or skill – as the humanitarian design community according to them promotes – is not enough for people truly gaining the 'capability to design'. The latter may, for example, be inhibited by political factors even though design skills are present.

Looking ahead: practical implementation

So far the idea presented in this chapter, of applying the capability approach to technological design, has hardly been implemented yet. Fortunately many designers are not oblivious to the considerations that a capability approach of design would highlight; in fact they regularly already take these into account without using the capability approach's vocabulary. Yet using the capability approach could make these design considerations more explicit and therefore more open to scrutiny and debate. The previous sections have hinted at possible benefits of more explicitly applying the capability approach to design, but of course the proof of the pudding is in the eating. That is where it is still lacking. Theorizing on the capability approach and design has only just begun and practical experience with it is still limited. One of the challenges is – so my interactions with some designers have indicated – that the conceptual framework of the capability approach is not immediately obvious and takes a little effort to learn. One possible solution – one that will appeal to practical people like designers – would be to develop checklists, tools and methods based on the capability approach that designers could use in different phases of the design process. So far, these do not exist. For other members of the 'design for values' family implementation has already received much more attention. There is a lot to be gained from looking in more detail into the tools and methods of design movements which share some ideals and insights with the capability approach, such as participatory design and inclusive/universal design.

However, applying tools should become no replacement for genuine critical reflection. Take for example 'design for sustainability', one of the areas in which quantitative tools have already become available. Various software packages exist that help designers to make a qualitative life cycle analysis of their product. This comes, however, with the risk of an uncritical usage and an unhelpful simplification of the issues and dilemmas at hand. In response a chapter in one of the major textbooks on engineering ethics (Brumsen 2011) warns that these programmes may create an unjustified air of simplicity. They weigh and add different environmental aspects into one final number. Thus the software's outcomes are based on the normative considerations of the programmers and a specific way of aggregating different considerations. These may subsequently not become a topic of discussion among designers. Even more qualitatively oriented life cycle approaches, Brumsen points out, still have the disadvantage of focusing on environmental impact, while leaving other aspects of sustainability, such as intergenerational justice, unaddressed. One could say that the idea of sustainability and of a flourishing human life share the problem of multidimensionality. Both may give rise to dilemmas during design – and these may need to be addressed explicitly, based on the problem, context or case at hand. Regarding the operationalization of the capability approach in general, Alkire (2005: 127) has argued that

> operationalizing it is not a one-time thing ... many of the residual value judgments in the capability approach will need to be made on the ground over and over again ... For example, no one 'list' of basic capabilities will be relevant to every evaluation or assessment or measurement exercise or index: the selection of functionings or capabilities upon which to focus will need to be done repeatedly. The same might apply to principles ... operationalization needs to occur not only in many countries, but also at many different levels, and in respect to different problems.

This means that the availability of a plurality of methods and tools is desirable.

One such attempt at operationalization of the capability approach is a recent, still ongoing project at Delft University of Technology to develop an

Opportunity Detection Kit for 'design for development' projects (Mink *et al.* 2014; Van der Marel 2012). Mink *et al.* (2014: 2) notice that

> several valuable design methods and toolkits have [already] been developed for NGOs, social enterprises or community workers of which most provide guidelines on how to develop an interview approach, how to establish appropriate questions, and how to question people, and IDEO does provide example discussion guides with questions, but they do not specify explicitly which topics to discuss or which questions to ask. This is left to the designer or the design team.

Their Opportunity Detection Kit is based on an extensive list of possibly relevant capabilities drawn from the literature. It includes among others 'sensitizing cards' to visualize these and make them part of the conversation with users. It therefore attempts to give somewhat more guidance on the possible development or well-being impacts of the design project in question, while also keeping the conversation open enough. In its current form it is meant to assist a designer to evaluate an existing product from the perspective of the capability approach, in interaction with the user, and detect opportunities for further design and development. At other places as well people have started to experiment with applying the capability approach to design. For example, Leydens *et al.* (2014) have given it a central role in their perspective on 'design for social justice', which they use in engineering education at the Colorado School of Mines and the Rensselaer Polytechnic Institute. It will be interesting to see how such initiatives further develop. The next chapter will explore in more detail the importance of paying attention to not only the details of design, but also to the socio-technical embedding of new technologies. Ideally, these should not be separate exercises. Rather, an iterative movement is needed between 'zooming in' on the details of design and 'zooming out' to consider the socio-technical embedding – which need to be considered in an integral way.

Notes

1. Most of this section is adapted from Oosterlaken (2013: ch. 7).
2. As quoted by Van den Hoven (2012: 32).
3. Not all of them are referring to the capability approach though.
4. This discussion of the bicycle example has been adapted from Oosterlaken (2009).
5. The next sections are – with some modifications and extensions – based on Oosterlaken (2014).

6 Note though that 'the value-ladenness of technology can be construed in a host of different ways' (Franssen et al. 2009).
7 In the partial theory of justice that Nussbaum has proposed in her work, it is posed that each and every individual should have each of the ten capabilities on her list up to a certain threshold level.
8 Unfortunately, the literature available on the case does not reveal whether the design indeed led to a sustainable entrepreneurial success.
9 Capability scholars acknowledge furthermore that there are several reasons why a focus on functionings instead of capabilities may sometimes be justified for evaluative purposes (Robeyns 2005).
10 Brey (2006) reports that the USA apparently made this mechanism mandatory for all car manufacturers for a short period in the 1970s.'U.S. car drivers', he says, 'did not appreciate being mechanically forced to wear their seatbelts, and many drivers had the mechanism illegally removed. Some people even mounted a court challenge: they felt that the coercive mechanism went against their civil liberties. As a result of these protests, the law was repealed, and wearing seatbelts became again something that was mandatory but no longer mechanically forced.'

References

Alkire, S. (2005). Why the Capability Approach? *Journal of Human Development* 6(1):115–33.

Atkinson, B.M.C. (2006). Captology: A Critical Review. In: IJsselsteijn, W., De Kort, Y., Midden, C., Eggen, B. and Van den Hoven, E. (eds), *Persuasive 2006*. Eindhoven: Springer, pp. 171–82.

Basalla, G. (1989). *The Evolution of Technology*. Cambridge: Cambridge University Press.

Bazoli, G. (2011). Designing an educative program about menstrual symptoms and a sanitary napkin life-cycle redesign for rural Indian women. Delft: Delft University of Technology (master's thesis, http://repository.tudelft.nl/view/ir/uuid% 3A90c6b5e6-89a3-42df-b5f4-a030c1d5a919 [accessed 11 September 2014]).

Berdichevsky, D. and Neuenschwander, E. (1999). Toward an Ethics of Persuasive Technology. In: *Communications of the ACM*.

Bijker, W.E. (1995). *Of Bicycles, Bakelites, and Bulbs; Toward a Theory of Sociotechnical Change*. Cambridge, MA: MIT Press.

Brey, P. (2006). Ethical Aspects of Behavior-Steering Technology. In: Verbeek, P.-P.C.C. and Slob, A. (eds), *User Behavior and Technology Development; Shaping Sustainable Relations Between Consumers and Technologies*. Dordrecht: Springer.

Brumsen, M. (2011). Sustainability, Ethics and Technology. In: Van de Poel, I. and Royakkers, L. (eds), *Ethics, Technology and Engineering*. Malden/Oxford: Wiley-Blackwell.

Buchanan, R. (2001). Human Dignity and Human Rights: Thoughts on the Principles of Human-Centered Design. *Design Issues* 17(3):35–9.

Coeckelbergh, M. (2011). Human Development or Human Enhancement? A Methodological Reflection on Capabilities and the Evaluation of Information Technologies. *Ethics and Information Technology* 13(2):81–92.

Comim, F. (2008). Measuring Capabilities. In: Comim, F., Qizilbash, M. and Alkire, S. (eds), *The Capability Approach; Concepts, Measures and Applications*. Cambridge: Cambridge University Press.

Connell, B.R. and Sanford, J.A. (1999). Research Implications of Universal Design. In: Steinfeld, E. and Danford, G.S. (eds), *Enabling Environments: Measuring the Impact of Environment on Disability and Rehabilitation*. New York: Kluwer Academic.

Davis, J. (2009). Design Methods for Ethical Persuasive Computing. In: *Persuasive 2009*. ACM International Conference Proceeding Series, Claremont, California, USA.

Dong, A. (2008). The Policy of Design: A Capabilities Approach. *Design Issues* 24(4):76–87.

Flanagan, M., Howe, D.C. and Nissenbaum, H. (2008). Embodying Values in Technology: Theory and Practice. In: Van den Hoven, J. and Weckert, J. (eds), *Information Technology and Moral Philosophy*. Cambridge: Cambridge University Press, pp. 322–53.

Fogg, B.J. (2003). *Persuasive Technology: Using Computers to Change What We Think and Do*. San Francisco, CA: Morgan Kaufmann Publishers.

Franssen, M. *et al*. (2009). Philosophy of Technology. *Stanford Encyclopedia of Philosophy* (spring 2009 edition). E.N. Zalta. Online: http://plato.stanford.edu/entries/technology (accessed 5 March 2014).

Frediani, A.A. and Boano, C. (2012). Processes for Just Products: The Capability Space of Participatory Design. In: Oosterlaken, I. and Van den Hoven, J. (eds), *The Capability Approach, Technology and Design*. Dordrecht: Springer.

Friedman, B. and Kahn, P.H.J. (2003). Human Values, Ethics and Design. In: Jacko, J. and Sears, A. (eds), *Handbook of Human–Computer Interaction*. Mahwah, NJ: Lawrence Erlbaum, pp. 1177–201.

Illies, C. and Meijers, A. (2014). Artefacts, Agency and Action Schemes. In: Kroes, P. and Verbeek, P.-P. (eds), *Technical Artefacts and Moral Agency*. Dordrecht: Springer.

Johnstone, J. (2007). Technology as Empowerment: A Capability Approach to Computer Ethics. *Ethics and Information Technology* 9(1):73–87.

—— (2012). Capabilities. In: P. Brey, A. Briggle and E. Spence (eds), *The Good Life in a Technological Age*. Abingdon, Oxon.: Routledge.

Kandachar, P., Diehl, J.C., Parmar, V.S. and Shivarama, C.K. (2011). *Designing with Emerging Markets – Design of Products and Services (2011 Edition)*. Delft: Delft University of Technology.

Kandachar, P., Diehl, J.C., Van Leeuwen, G. and Daalhuizen, J. (eds) (2007). Design of Products and Services for the Base of the Pyramid; IDE Graduation Projects 2. Delft: Delft University of Technology, Faculty of Industrial Design Engineering.

Keates, S. (2014). Designing for Inclusivity. In: Van den Hoven, J., Vermaas, P.E. and Van de Poel, I. (eds), *Handbook of Ethics, Values and Technological Design*. Dordrecht: Springer.

Kleine, D., Light, A. and Montero, M.-J. (2012). Signifiers of the Life We Value? – Considering Human Development, Technologies and Fair Trade from the Perspective of the Capabilities Approach. *Information Technology for Development* 18(1):42–60.

Lawson, C. (2010). Technology and the Extension of Human Capabilities. *Journal for the Theory of Social Behaviour* 40(2):207–23.

Leydens, J.A., Lucena, J.A. and Nieusma, D. (2014). What is design for social justice? Paper presented at the 121st ASEE Annual Conference & Exposition, Indianapolis, IN, 15–18 June.

Lockton, D., Harisson, D. and Stanton, N. (2008). Making the User More Efficient: Design for Sustainable Behaviour. *International Journal of Sustainable Engineering* 1(1).

Mink, A., Van der Marel, F., Parmar, V. and Kandachar, P. (2014). Using the Capability Approach to Detect Design Opportunities. In: *Design for Sustainable Wellbeing and Empowerment*. Bangalore, India.

Murphy, C. and Gardoni, P. (2012). Design, Risk and Capabilities. In: Oosterlaken, I. and Van den Hoven, J. (eds), *The Capability Approach, Technology and Design*. Dordrecht: Springer.

Narayan, D., Chambers, R., Shah, M. K. and Petesch, P. (2000). *Voices of the Poor: Crying Out for Change*. Published for the World Bank, New York: Oxford University Press.

Nichols, C. and Dong, A. (2012). Re-Conceptualizing Design through the Capability Approach. In: Oosterlaken, I. and Van den Hoven, J. (eds), *The Capability Approach, Technology & Design*. Dordrecht: Springer.

Nieusma, D. (2004). Alternative Design Scholarship: Working towards Appropriate Design. *Design Issues* 20(3):13–24.

Nissenbaum, H. (2005). Values in technical design. In Mitcham, C. (ed.), *Encyclopedia of Science, Technology, and Ethics*. Detroit, MI: Macmillan, pp. 66–70.

Nussbaum, M.C. (2000). *Women and Human Development: The Capability Approach*. New York: Cambridge University Press.

Nussbaum, M.C. (2006). *Frontiers of Justice; Disability, Nationality, Species Membership*. Cambridge, MA: Belknap Press of Harvard University Press.

Nussbaum, M.C. (2012). Inappropriate Artefact, Unjust Design? Human Diversity as a Key Concern in the Capability Approach and Inclusive Design. In: Oosterlaken, I. and Van den Hoven, J. (eds), *The Capability Approach, Technology and Design*. Dordrecht: Springer, pp. 223–44.

Nussbaum, M.C. (2013). Taking a capability approach to technology and its design – a philosophical exploration (doctoral dissertation), vol. 8. Simon Stevin Series in the Ethics of Technology (edited by Brey, Philip; Kroes, Peter; Meijers, Anthonie). 3TU. Centre for Ethics and Technology, Delft.

Nussbaum, M.C. (2014). Human Capabilities in Design for Values. In: Van den Hoven, J., Van de Poel, I. and Vermaas, P.E. (eds), *Handbook of Ethics, Values and Technological Design*. Dordrecht: Springer.

Ortega y Gasset, J. (1961). Man the technician. In Ortega y Gasset, J. (ed.), *History as a System*. New York: Norton Library.

Ortega y Gasset, J. (1972). Thoughts on Technology (translated by Helene Weyl). In: Mitcham, C. and Mackey, R. (eds), *Philosophy and Technology: Readings in the Philosophical Problems of Technology*. New York: Free Press.

Otte, P.P. (2014). Developing Technology: The Quest for a New Theoretical Framework for Understanding the role of Technology in Human Development. *Technology in Society* 38(0):11–17.

Parmar, V., Keyson, D. and De Bont, C. (2008). Persuasive Technology for Shaping Social Beliefs of Rural Women in India: An Approach Based on the Theory of

Planned Behaviour. In: H. Oinas.-Kukkonen *et al.* (eds), *Persuasive 2008*. Oulu, Finland: Springer, pp. 104–15.

Radder, H. (2009). Why Technologies are Inherently Normative. In: Meijers, A. (ed.), *Handbook of the Philosophy of Technology and Engineering Sciences*. Amsterdam, Reed Elsevier. pp. 887–922.

Rawls, J. (1999). *A Theory of Justice (Revised Edition)*. Cambridge, MA: Harvard University Press.

Robeyns, I. (2000). An Unworkable Idea or a Promising Alternative? Sen's Capability Approach Re-examined. *Center for Economic Studies Discussion paper 00.30*. Leuven: Katholieke Universiteit Leuven.

Robeyns, I. (2005). The Capability Approach – A Theoretical Survey. *Journal of Human Development* 6(1):94–114.

Robeyns, I. (2011). The Capability Approach. In: Zalta, E. N. (ed.), *Stanford Encyclopedia of Philosophy*.

Sen, A. (1985). *Commodities and Capabilities*. Amsterdam/New York: North-Holland.

Steen, M. (2011). Tensions in Human-Centred Design. *CoDesign* 7(1):45–60.

Van de Poel, I. (2009). Values in Engineering Design. In: Meijers, A. (ed.), *Handbook of the Philosophy of Science. Volume 9: Philosophy of Technology and Engineering Sciences*. Oxford: Elsevier, pp. 973–1006.

Van de Poel, I. (2012). Can We Design for Well-being? In: Brey, P., Briggle, A. and Spence, E. (eds), *The Good Life in a Technological Age*. New York: Routledge.

Van de Poel, I. (2013). Translating values into design requirements. In: Mitchfelder, D., McCarty, N. and Goldberg, D.E. (eds), *Philosophy and Engineering: Reflections on Practice, Principles and Process*. Dordrecht: Springer, pp. 253–66.

Van de Poel, I. (forthcoming). *Design and Well-being*. Delft: Delft University of Technology.

Van den Hoven, J. (2007). ICT and Value Sensitive Design. In: Goujon, P., Lavelle, S., Duquenoy, P., Kimppa, K. and Laurent, V. (eds), *The Information Society: Innovations, Legitimacy, Ethics and Democracy*. Boston, MA: Springer, pp. 67–72.

Van den Hoven, J. (2012a). Neutrality and Technology: Ortega Y Gasset on the Good Life. In: Brey, P., Briggle, A. and Spence, E. (eds), *The Good Life in a Technological Age*. Abingdon, Oxon.: Routledge.

Van den Hoven, J. (2012b). Human Capabilities and Technology. In: Oosterlaken, I. and Van den Hoven, J. (eds), *The Capability Approach, Technology and Design*. Dordrecht: Springer.

Van den Hoven, J., Van de Poel, I. and Vermaas, P.E. (eds) (2014). *Handbook of Ethics, Values and Technological Design*. Dordrecht: Springer.

Van der Marel, F. (2012). Developing an impact evaluation framework for product designers inspired by the capability approach: a case study on the Philips Chulha. M.Sc. thesis, Delft University of Technology.

Verbeek, P.-P.C.C. (2008). Morality in Design: Design Ethics and the Morality of Technological Artifacts. In: Vermaas, P.E., Kroes, P., Light, A. and Moore, S.A. (eds), *Philosophy and Design; From Engineering to Architecture*. Heidelberg: Springer.

Winner, L. (1980). Do Artifacts Have Politics? *Daedalus* 109(1):121–36.

Ziegler, R. (2010). Innovations in Doing and Being: Capability Innovations at the

Intersection of Schumpeterian Political Economy and Human Development. *Journal of Social Entrepreneurship* 1(2):255–72.

Ziegler, R., Karanja, B. and Dietsche, C. (2013). Toilet Monuments: An Investigation of Innovation for Human Development. *Journal of Human Development and Capabilities* 14(3):420–40.

3
EMBEDDING TECHNOLOGY IN SOCIO-TECHNICAL NETWORKS

The social nature of individual human capabilities

Understanding the relation between technical artefacts and individual human capabilities requires us to regularly move back and forth between 'zooming in' on the details of an artefact's design, and 'zooming out' to grasp the socio-technical embedding of the artefact in question. This chapter will reflect on the latter.[1] However, it is useful to first scrutinize the nature of individual human capabilities in some more detail. What will be argued in this section is that individual human capabilities as valued by the capability approach are actually thoroughly social or relational by nature. The second section will then discuss how technical artefacts can be inserted in this picture of human capabilities. Or put stronger: how they *need* to be given a place in this social perspective, as technical artefacts by their nature cannot fulfil the intended function of expanding human capabilities without being properly embedded in socio-technical networks. Next, some implications will be explored, the most important of which is that the concept of 'conversion factors' has its limitations in helping us understand how a technical artefact can be made to contribute to the expansion of capabilities. The last part of the chapter will discuss that it is possible to come to different assessments of the effect of socio-technical networks on individual freedom. Before any of that, however, this section will first discuss the social nature of individual capabilities.

That *individual* human capabilities are the focal point of the capability approach has in the past been a point of scholarly debate. While acknowledging the moral importance of individual capabilities, some development scholars have argued that the strong emphasis that the capability approach puts on them masks or downplays the importance of groups and social structures in the development process.[2] Criticisms along this line have among others been voiced by Stewart (2005) and Ibrahim (2006). Ibrahim in her paper wishes to 'point out the limitations of the capability approach in capturing the interactive relationship between individual capabilities and social structures' (p. 397). In order to address this weakness, she proposes to combine the capability approach with various other literatures, especially those on collective action, institutions and social capital. Ibrahim's criticism is a specific instantiation of a point that has been made a number of times in the preceding chapters – namely that the capability approach, as a general conceptual framework, is not able to tell us much, if anything at all, about all sorts of phenomena in our empirical reality which shape individual capabilities. This includes phenomena like technology, gender, the formation of people's preferences and indeed also social structures. Another paper on this topic, by Stewart (2005), asserts that 'groups play a much more dominant role in human life and well-being than appears in much of the analysis of capabilities' (p. 185). She describes various ways in which groups, such as credit associations for poor women or ethnic groups, can be both beneficial and harmful for individuals. Stewart argues that group capabilities deserve more attention, and that they need to be included in analyses along with individual capabilities.

A useful distinction to keep in mind when engaging in this debate is that between ontological, methodological and ethical individualism, a distinction that Robeyns (2005) applies to the capability approach. Methodological or explanatory individualism is 'the view that everything can be explained by reference to individuals and their properties only'. Ontological individualism 'states that only individuals and their properties exist, and that all social entities and properties can be identified by reducing them to individuals and their properties' (p. 108). So according to this view society is not more than the sum of individuals. Ethical individualism, Robeyns argues, is a claim that 'individuals, and only individuals, are the [ultimate] units of moral concern' (p. 107). Groups and social structures then become relevant only to the degree that they benefit or harm individuals. Robeyns (2005) concludes that the capability approach is committed to ethical individualism – more specifically to the agency and well-being of each and every individual. However, according to her it does not make sense to understand the capability approach as a methodologically or ontologically individualistic approach. Indeed, as Robeyns (2005) points out, there does exist work that is based on the capability approach and that pays attention to groups and social structures. Whether this amounts to *sufficient* attention, she sharply notices, is a value judgement and not a factual one. What this work shows, however, is that the capability approach is in principle able to embrace or incorporate the role of groups and social structures in the expansion of individual capabilities.[3]

Digging a little deeper, a question that one may want to ask is how exactly capabilities arise in the interaction between individuals and social structures. 'Are elements of the context to be treated as external variables that somehow enhance capabilities?', Smith and Seward (2009: 214) wonder. 'Or are they actually a constitutive part of capabilities themselves?' It seems that the latter is more in line with how Sen and Nussbaum view the approach. Nussbaum (2000) makes a distinction between the innate and internal capacities of a person on the one hand, and so-called 'combined capabilities', on the other. The ability to see is such an innate capacity, and literacy is an example of an internal capacity – one that needs to be developed. Combined capabilities, Nussbaum says, come about when innate/internal capacities are combined with 'suitable external conditions for the exercise of the functioning in question' (p. 85). These conditions include social structures. For example a person may be literate, but does not have the effective freedom or capability to read unless reading materials are available, prohibitive cultural norms do not prevent her from reading, and so on. The individual's capability to read will be bigger in a society where social structures such as libraries exist. As the capability approach is concerned with what people are realistically able to do and be in life, it takes such combined capabilities to be the ultimate ends of development interventions.

Similarly, Smith and Seward (2009) argue that the ontology that is implicit in Sen's many writings is contextual and relational. In this perspective individual capabilities depend on individual-level capacities on the one hand and the individual's relative position within social structures on the other hand.[4] Examples of such social structures are gangs, churches and governments. One can thus look at structures at smaller and more encompassing levels. In their article Smith and Seward set out to explicate this view at the rather abstract level of philosophical ontology – more specifically a critical realist ontology.[5] Following Martins (2006, 2007), they argue that social structures have certain causal powers which emerge from the internal relations of their constituent parts – mainly people. This particular constitution of the social structure can operate in certain ways – mechanisms which reveal themselves as these causal powers. Such causal mechanisms do not operate in a deterministic way, considering the multitude of interacting mechanisms in our highly complex world. They are 'better understood as *tendencies* of a structure to behave in a particular way' (Smith and Seward: 217). The idea (p. 218) is that the conventional notion of causality ('if *a*, then *b*') is replaced with a 'contextual causality' in the sense of '*x* causes *y* (in circumstances *c*)'. Individual capabilities are interpreted as a type of causal powers in this view. They also arise from 'structures with particular internal relations from which their causal powers ... emerge'. When activated, the causal mechanisms of such a structure lead to certain outcome: functionings which are realized. To conclude, the individual human capabilities that the capability approach takes an interest in often do not fully reside in the person, but are actually thoroughly social or relational in nature.

Inserting technical artefacts in the picture

The previous section briefly sketched the relational ontology that is arguably implicitly presupposed in the capability approach. Social scientists often only discuss people as the elements of which social structures are composed, so it is not surprising that Smith and Seward (2009) do not pay any attention to technology. The question that will be discussed in this section is how technology can be given a place in this picture – or rather *needs* to be given a place in this relational and contextual picture. The previous chapter already argued that technical artefacts generally only expand human capabilities when combined with certain shared usage practices. However, it is also the other way around: many of our social practices are only made possible by and are even partly shaped by technical artefacts. Technologies also contribute to human capabilities in ways which are more complex and structural. Think of how various technologies are indispensible for the functioning of many contemporary social structures, such as national health care systems or energy suppliers. These social structures are not only composed of people, but of people and technical artefacts – as is suggested by the term 'socio-technical systems'. The discussion in this section of how technical artefacts fit in the picture might stimulate some social scientists to start considering technology as a component of human capabilities that deserves explicit attention – a point which will of course not be surprising to scholars in specialized fields like science and technology studies (STS). However, this section first and foremost serves to make clear to engineers and technologists how important it is that attention be paid not just to the details of design of technical artefacts, but also to their socio-technical embedding.

For the purposes of this section an article by Lawson (2010), a philosopher of technology, is very helpful. His article does not refer to the capability approach of Nussbaum and Sen, but his view of human capabilities seems to be very much in line with it.[6] Lawson's main argument is that it is a defining characteristic of technical artefacts – setting them apart from toys, works of art and the like – that they extend human capabilities in a certain way.[7] He argues that technical artefacts will only expand human capabilities if they are incorporated in both 'technical and social networks of interdependencies'. He calls upon actor–network theory (ANT),[8] one of the most prominent approaches in the field of STS, to articulate this idea. 'Perhaps the central proposition of ANT,' he holds, 'is that technical objects cannot be understood in isolation. Rather technical objects take on their properties, characteristics, powers or whatever only in relation to the networks of relations in which they stand' (p. 212). The networks in which artefacts are enrolled have both social and material components. The example of the car can illustrate this. Basically a car remains just a specific configuration of wires, metal, nuts and bolts, and so on, until it is embedded in a network with roads, gas stations, traffic rules, driving schools, and the like. Only in such a network could the artefact be fully understood as a car, with all the powers that cars have. And, Lawson would arguably say, only then will it be substantially expanding people's capabilities to move about. Recall also the bicycle example discussed in the Introduction, including the observation that the presence of paved roads and the absence of prohibitive cultural norms matters for the bicycle's impact on human capabilities. A telephone can also illustrate the importance of the network in which an artefact is enrolled:

> A new phone must be inserted within technical networks where it has access to the right kind of telephone signal or the correct voltage of electricity, etc., but to be usable it must also be inserted within particular [social] relations, which might mean being left outside the house for Amish communities or it might assume the status of a best friend for a chatty teenager.
>
> *(Lawson 2010: 213)*

Lawson (2010: 214) argues that 'some aspects of the technical object can be treated in exactly the same way as social structure … for the simple reason that the social relations, in which artefacts stand, are constitutive of the artefact' (as illustrated by the previous examples).

However, technical artefacts in one respect differ from social structures, Lawson argues. And this is that they have a dual nature, both a social and a material one. This becomes clear when we start looking into the interaction between individuals, social structures and artefacts through time. Individuals and social structures, at least in the philosophical ontology underlying the articles of both Smith and Seward (2009) and Lawson (2011), recursively depend on each other. In this ontology the link between social structures and individual agency or capabilities is to be found in so-called 'positioned practices': individuals engage in social practices and structures, in which they occupy certain positions. The exact position that a person has within and vice versa the social structures within a society, Smith and Seward (2009: 223) argue, 'subjects them to the causal mechanisms that constrain and enable behaviour'. To people it seems that the social structures in which they are embedded are an objective,[9] given reality. Yet, Smith and Seward (2009: 223) say, 'through human activities, [they] transform or reproduce social structures' over time.

But unlike social structures, technology is, says Lawson, 'not simply transformed or reproduced' through human activity:

> If human society disappears overnight hammers, in an important sense not shared by the highway-code, language, etc., do not. To be clear, what persists is the physical presence of the hammer, not its *being* a hammer, which of course is a construction that would indeed disappear along with human societies.
>
> *(Lawson 2010: 214)*

Social objects like passports or banknotes, says Lawson, mainly have causal powers that are relational. These powers depend on our shared beliefs and practices. In contrast, what defines technical objects like cars and hammers is that their primary causal powers are intrinsic to them. This difference between technical artefacts and social structures thus provides a reason to distinguish them as a separate constitutive element of human capabilities. Lawson (2010: 215) suggests that 'technical objects can be understood as "slotting" into positions in much the way that individuals do'. But they do have material properties (like being hard or heavy and subject to gravity) that humans by necessity cannot ignore. We have to come to terms with these mechanisms, Lawson claims. He argues that 'the positions into which technical objects "slot", are reproduced and transformed as human agents attempt to harness the causal powers of such objects' (Lawson 2010: 217). Technical activity (ranging from design to use), Lawson (2010: 217) proposes, is 'that activity that harnesses the intrinsic causal powers of material artefacts in order to extend human capabilities'.

Lawson's understanding of individual capabilities seems to be compatible with that of the capability approach on an ontological level. Yet it is worth noting that there is a difference in the way in which capabilities tend to be discussed in philosophy of technology and STS on the one hand and the capability approach on the other. The example of so-called 'sleeping policemen' or speed bumps which force people to drive slowly, can illustrate this. Philosophers of technology, Lawson notes, tend to discuss such cases in terms of technology 'disciplining' drivers into certain behaviour, thus 'imposing' a certain morality or ethics on them. Lawson instead chooses to highlight that such cases involve a direct expansion of human capabilities; the traffic authorities gain causal powers by introducing the sleeping policemen into the existing material and social network. This expands the capabilities of their officers at the expense of those of the drivers, whose capability to speed gets diminished. As the primary interest of the capability approach is in those valuable capabilities needed to live the life one has reason to value, this approach would rather highlight that the sleeping policemen contribute to traffic safety, which means that – in a more indirect way – the capabilities of citizens in the areas of bodily integrity and life get expanded. The capability of traffic officers to control drivers' behaviour makes this possible, but does not seem to have any intrinsic value. Yet whether one is interested in the capability to speed, the capability to control some aspect of other people's behaviour, or a capability to remain uninjured in traffic, they are comparable on the level of philosophical ontology. Although they may invoke very different ethical evaluations, these capabilities are all constituted by individuals, technical artefacts and social structures.

Exploring some implications

The first section has made clear that an individual is always, as Smith and Seward (2009: 218) assert, part of a 'context of particular enabling (or disabling) mechanisms'. This means that if you want to increase people's capabilities, you have to make sure that the required mechanisms exist. And which mechanisms those are depends on the context. Smith and Seward are thus wary of best practices, as 'it is hard to imagine that one set of practices will work in all contexts' (p. 231). The same applies, the previous section argued, to technical artefacts. As Lawson points out (2010: 220), 'extending our capabilities [with the help of technical artefacts] commits us to, or encourages us to invest in, particular networks of interdependencies'. Some of the past cases of failed technology transfer to developing countries can serve as an illustration of the fact that technologies do not expand human capabilities without the required interdependencies between people, social structures and other artefacts being present in the recipient country. 'Best technologies' thus also is something we should be wary of, as the appropriate technology already pointed out decades ago (see Chapter 1). Furthermore, as the case of 'sleeping policemen' already hinted at:

> The introduction of a particular technology involves the extension of the capabilities of some, empowering them while making others disempowered or even redundant. Thus a central task will be to question whose capabilities ... are being extended, and what the implications of this might be.
>
> *(Lawson 2010: 220)*

Since the capability approach values the capabilities of each and every individual, a certain methodological individualism may thus – so Smith and Seward (2009) argue – be recommendable. The idea is (p. 228) that our 'analysis must focus on the relative positioning of the individuals within the social structure to understand for whom different structures are differentially causal' and thus for whom – for example – certain essential capabilities may sink under some acceptable threshold level. Also in the case of technology, one should sometimes resort to such methodological individualism in order to assess socio-technological arrangements on their merits for different categories of individuals.

The capability approach as a general conceptual framework of course does not tell us how to effectively embed technical artefacts in socio-technical networks, nor how socio-technical changes affect the distribution of capabilities over different categories of individuals. From fields such as STS we should borrow those theories, approaches and methods that can increase our understanding of these matters. For example, Zheng and Stahl (2011, 2012) have argued that combining the capability approach with critical theory, as employed in STS and information systems research, would be a useful supplement. The interaction between technical and social aspects is central to this body of work. It deals in an explicit and direct way with the relation between technology and the distribution of power, Zheng and Stahl note – something which is according to them lacking in the capability approach. One obvious example where such issues of power are at stake are technologies for digital rights management, used by publishers and hardware producers to control the use of devices and their digital content after sale. At the same time Zheng and Stahl judge that critical technology theorists sometimes get stuck in their attempt to 'debunk positive myths' about technology by continuously pointing out how technology is implied in the distribution of power and sometimes even in outright oppression. The capability approach is then useful to draw attention to the potential positive impact of technology on the expansion of valuable capabilities. It can pay a constructive role by 'asking questions about what conversion factors need to be in place to facilitate the achievement of potential freedom that technology provides' (p. 77). Analytic exercises of 'isolating' or 'highlighting' certain categories of individuals from the network may clarify the specific conversion factors at work for these people. And sometimes designers may be able, it was argued in the previous chapter, to proactively and successfully take such conversion factors into account.

Although the notion of personal, social and environmental conversion factors is abundantly present in the capability approach literature, and numerous examples are mentioned, more critical reflection on the notion might be useful. It does not seem to be a fundamental ontological category, in the sense that there exists a class of phenomena in the world that *are* conversion factors independently from our analyses. Something rather gets the status or label 'conversion factor' in an analysis that zooms in on the relation between some resource on the one hand and some individual capability on the other hand. The capability approach criticizes an evaluative focus on resources because they often do not convert into capabilities for everybody. A list of 'conversion factors' then presents an accessible overview of causes for the variability in the relation. At the same time such a list is a flattening or simplification of the network of interdependencies between people and artefacts that is behind the presence or absence of capabilities for certain (categories of) individuals.[10] Take a case which was briefly mentioned in the previous chapter: tricycles being redesigned for disabled people in Ghana, in such a way that they could sell products like ice-cream from the cooler installed at the front. To make this development a success it was investigated how to embed this artefact in a larger network, also involving a local metal workshop being able to produce and repair the tricycles, a supplier of products to be sold, and so on.[11] It is possible to list 'absence of ice-cream supplier' as a problematic conversion factor that mediates the relation between the tricycles and the capability to earn a livelihood. Yet effectively addressing such conversion factors in development practice may often require getting an understanding of the full network in all its complexities. For example, even if there is such a supplier – will the target group have access to the micro-credit that they may need to acquire products? Moreover not all elements of the network of interdependencies that need to be in place for a *durable* expansion of capabilities may sensibly be captured as a conversion factor with regard to some resource–capability relationship. The metal workshop able to do maintenance and repairs may be such an example. It is a precondition for keeping the tricycles fully functioning in the long term, rather than a factor influencing the conversion of resource into capability. In short, rather than asking what conversion factors need to be taken care of, a better question to ask may be which network of interdependencies needs to be in place.

An interesting analysis along the same lines is provided by Kullman and Lee (2012), who argue that 'designed materials are not converted by individuals or even humans alone, but by situated arrangements of people, technologies and environments' (p. 50). They discuss the One Laptop per Child (OLPC) programme as an illustrative case. This programme aimed to develop low-priced laptops (< $100) with bespoke software, and have governments in developing countries distribute it on a massive scale to children aged 6–12. Kullman and Lee (p. 46) note that the promotion material from the OLPC programme shows that 'OLPC tends to equate laptop ownership with education'. In terms of the basic underlying view on technology and human development as discussed in Chapter 1, this programme thus falls in the category of the 'race to the universal fix' – one technology providing a worldwide solution to a major development challenge. According to Kullman and Lee the OLPC project puts the emphasis on self-teaching, where the child – through possession of the laptop – is supposed to transcend the limitations of her/his situation by educating her/himself. They note (p. 48) that

> OLPC seems to confuse 'freedom' with the use of laptops and the digital spaces of computer networks, therefore bypassing other important relations that make learning possible. The promotional materials rarely mention teachers, properly functioning school facilities and the social and educational importance of sharing learning equipment.

The question of how the laptops fit in with local curricula is apparently not really addressed by the programme, nor is there sufficient training for the teachers on how to use the laptops. Kullman and Lee refer to a number of empirical studies on the implementation of OLPC laptops in different countries which indicate that the conversion of the technical artefact into valuable capabilities does depend on the nature and quality of the socio-technical embedding. Yet personal, social and environmental conversion factors are hard to disentangle, Kullman and Lee conclude, 'as the implementation of laptops mobilizes a complex arrangement of teachers, children, classrooms, funding and infrastructures' (p. 51). Paying attention to such matters would mean that truly expanding valuable human capabilities with the help of the laptops becomes more of a 'slow race' rather than providing a quick fix.

If we consider technical artefacts outside their full context of implementation, we may thus not be able to get an adequate estimation of the degree to which they will truly enable people to lead a life they have reason to value. Another example can be found in a case described by Mink et al. (2014). It concerns the redesign of a silk reeling machine used in rural livelihood projects of an Indian development organization. In terms of the capability approach this project was expanding the women's basic capability to sustain themselves and their families. The new design contributed to this project goal by solving problems like energy-loss during reeling, failing materials and yarn-quality problems. The designer also addressed the safety and health issues which the old machine posed for the reeling women. So the new design improved their capabilities for bodily integrity and health. A further design requirement which was successfully addressed was for the machine to become smaller, lighter and movable. The old, heavy machine could only be used in the silk reeling centre. The new machine would in theory give the women the freedom to work either at home, or at the silk reeling centre. During a re-examination of the case some time after the implementation of the machines, it was however found that this is not how it worked out in practice. This was due to the local network of interdependencies in which the machines were implemented. According to the local cultural norms, women were supposed to stay home as much as possible. Now that it was possible to work from home, some women were no longer allowed to go to the silk reeling centre. This was a regrettable outcome, as many women actually appreciated being able to work in the reeling centres. It contributed to their capability of affiliation, being able to engage in meaningful and nourishing social relations – one of the central capabilities on Nussbaum's list. Moreover, the possibility to connect with other women in silk reeling centres is arguably not only intrinsically valuable, but also as a means towards their further empowerment. Despite extensive fieldwork the designer had overlooked this aspect of the project's development impact. An explicit consideration of the well-being of women in terms of Nussbaum's full list of capabilities during the design phase might have led to a different project outcome.

What has been argued in the preceding sections is that the effect of technical artefacts on human capabilities partly depends on the way they are embedded in broader socio-technical networks. The challenge that this poses may perhaps seem most salient in the context of developing countries, where even basic socio-technical networks and infrastructures are lacking. However, even in the North it may be a challenge to successfully implement new technical artefacts, as the case of introducing electric cars can illustrate. Although these vehicles have existed for some time now, we have still not seen a large-scale introduction because it is so complex to effectuate the required changes in the existing socio-technical system that is geared towards cars with a combustion engine. Geels (2004) for example identifies the fuel infrastructure – think about oil companies and petrol stations – as one element of the socio-technical system surrounding cars. Electric cars need places where they can recharge, but implementing an infrastructure for this purpose comes with many challenges. Until these are solved, even a well-designed electric car will not get used on a large scale. It seems therefore that the design of technical artefacts has only a limited role to play in effectuating positive change. This may raise some doubt about the possibility of 'design for capabilities' as discussed in the previous chapter. Chapter 2 already made clear that 'design for capabilities' is more complex and demanding than 'traditional' design approaches. It seems undeniable that there are substantive limits – including epistemological ones – to the degree to which designers can take responsibility for the effective creation of valuable human capabilities. They have after all only limited knowledge of and influence on the way their products will be embedded in wider socio-technical networks. This seems to be even more the case when we take into account the long-term and systemic effects of the introduction of new technologies, which may have an indirect effect on a range of valuable capabilities. One may therefore wonder if 'design for capabilities' is not just a very nice idea that is very difficult, if not impossible to put into practice. However, that the details of design may matter to some degree for the capability impact of new technologies seems just as undeniable as the limitations to the influence of design. The question of how important the influence of design is in comparison with other factors is not one that can be answered in the abstract, for 'technology' in general. From the empirical turn in philosophy of technology (Kroes and Meijers 2000) we can learn that such questions are best raised and answered for concrete technologies and contexts of applications. Doubts about the possibility of 'design for capabilities' however also raises a further issue, namely how we understand, organize and practise design. Leydens *et al.* (2014), having experimented with using the capability approach in 'design for social justice' projects within engineering education, ask the question whether it is wise to 'introduce excessive ambiguity and throw engineering student designers into highly unfamiliar interdisciplinary terrain' (p. 26). One possible answer, they notice, is that it is not helping future engineers to train them by using design problems that are artificially confined by ignoring the complex socio-technical context in which real design takes place and gets implemented. It can be argued, they say, that engineers are stimulated to learn about relevant socio-technical issues and from other disciplines exactly through engaging with rich design challenges that do address real issues of well-being, poverty and justice.

The system character of technology and individual freedom

Let us dig a little deeper into the possible implications of the basic idea that the power of technical artefacts to expand human capabilities depends on their embedment in socio-technical networks. This also means that socio-technical networks are transformed when new technologies are introduced. The specific question central in this section is what the implications are for the real and effective freedom of individuals to realize the sort of life they have reason to value. Broadly speaking, so a paper by Briggle (2009) argues, there are two lines of thinking conceivable. The first line of thinking is adopted by what Briggle has labelled 'pluralist theorists of technology'. Recall that the previous chapter discussed a triangular relation between technical artefacts, human capabilities and ideas of the good life. In a further step, usage or social practices were added to the picture, acknowledging that it is often the combination of technical artefact and social practice that leads to the expansion of human capabilities. It was also discussed that new views of the good life often arise together with new technological possibilities, for example the ideal of being a young urban professional which is facilitated by mobile phones and laptops. This 'extended triangle' (Figure 2.2) seems compatible with pluralist theories of technology. Pluralists admit that 'technologies shape identities and practices and are thus not neutral with respect to the good life' (Briggle: 7). Therefore, as was mentioned in the previous chapter, we need to reflect on the good life when developing and designing new technical artefacts. Yet pluralists hold that a variety of uses is possible for any technical artefact and they emphasize the freedoms that users have while engaging with technical artefacts or participating in certain technological practices. Moreover, different technologies can, according to this view, exist side by side. Thus they see a plurality of technologies as 'supporting a diversity of ways of being and conceptions of the good life while nonetheless shaping those ways of being and conceptions'.

Such pluralist views of technologies can be contrasted with views that are in line with the second way of thinking. Such views emphasize that technology has a very strong system character, and it is the type of view that Briggle himself favours. Such 'system views of technology' further complicate and extend the picture presented in Figure 2.2 (see Figure 3.1). Van den Hoven (2012: 335) for example also adopts this line of thinking. He argues that 'technology's typical service value' – or its power to expand capabilities – 'can only be enjoyed in networks of users, producers, and those who maintain, govern and disseminate it, and hence give it its real value'. So far this claim seems to add not much new to what was discussed in the previous sections, but philosophers of technology like Van den Hoven and Briggle argue that the implications have so far not been fully driven through. According to Van den Hoven 'all significant technology is public in a relevant sense', namely that one cannot keep it confined to small-scale socio-technical practices that one can always freely join or leave. In the system view, technology at least partly shapes our life-world in a way that is beyond the individual that freely chooses to engage in certain practices. Contrary to the assumptions made by pluralist views of technology, Briggle (2009: 5) likewise holds, 'the impacts of technology cannot be so easily privatized and controlled. Indeed, the technological patterning of life occurs in a way that no one freely chooses.' Recall the example of a car, the effect of which on people's capability to move about depends on the surrounding socio-technical system, which includes roads, gas stations, traffic rules, driving schools, and the like. Briggle takes this idea even further. He asserts (p. 5) that cars

> do not just transport people in an otherwise unchanged world; they shape infrastructures, create markets, alter residential patterns and communities, and influence, through their use of oil and other materials, international relations and the global environment. Furthermore, in

shaping the character of the human life world, they play a role in both generating and foreclosing lifestyle choices.

For example the system of roads extending to remote places, Briggle judges, 'does foreclose the opportunity of a solitary hike in those places and it does create a new networked existence for those brought within the sphere of influence of the roads'. As a society we may need to decide on the question whether the capability for solitary hikes is more important for a good human life than the capability to quickly and easily drive anywhere, or whether we are somehow able to guarantee both capabilities up to some threshold level. The necessity and urgency for collective deliberation about technology and the good life becomes stronger if one adopts a system view of technology. Yet such deliberation does not solve the fundamental problem that an individual living in contemporary high-tech society is perhaps not as free in his life choices as pluralist views of technology assume.

These very rough sketches of these two complicated views, which could each be worked out in different ways, of course raise many further questions. One critical remark that one may want to make is that technical artefacts like cars clearly do not fully determine how society develops, and the capability impacts of their introduction depend on the specific way in which such

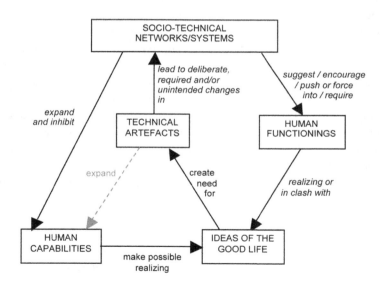

Figure 3.1 The system view of technology further complicating the triangle

artefacts become embedded in socio-technical networks. For example, the introduction of the car has arguably shaped the way in which urban areas in the USA have developed. As a result, it is often quite difficult to do commuting and shopping by bicycle, even though some may consider this as a healthier and more stress-free way of living. Yet the Netherlands is a very bicycle-friendly country, in which many people use the bicycle for shopping and commuting, even though car possession is also widespread. Strong technological determinism, the view that technological development is an autonomous force which subsequently determines societal development, is thus not tenable. If it were, there would be no possibility for us to influence such processes of change. And collective deliberation on technology, capabilities and the good life would be pointless then (except as an intellectual exercise). It should be noted though that there is a wide range of views possible between the extremes of full technological determinism, and full social determinism in which technology is merely a neutral tool towards human ends (see e.g. Radder 2009; Wyatt 2008). It would be a mistake to think that technology itself does not really matter. Despite disagreements about the details, most contemporary scholars in the fields of philosophy of technology and STS agree that the choice of technology co-shapes societal developments. For example, in a seminal article Winner (1980) has argued that energy technologies like solar panels are 'more compatible with a democratic, egalitarian society than energy systems based on coal, oil, and nuclear power' (p. 130). Especially the latter seem more prone to give rise to more authoritarian, centralized regimes because of the security and safety risks that need to be dealt with in the process of keeping the technology functioning. And as argued in the previous chapter, even the details of design may matter.

Another response to the system view could be that it really underestimates the freedoms or choices that we have as a car driver. Briggle admits (p. 8) that of course 'a system of roads does not force someone to travel in any particular direction'. His analysis (p. 7) is that 'the pluralists [of technology] are able to draw different conclusions due to their commitment to analyse technologies as discreet artefacts and practices without positing any emergent patterns on a larger scale'. The issue is not only at which level to execute our empirical analyses, but also at which level of abstraction to execute our normative evaluations. Capabilities could range from very concrete to very abstract. For example, we could sensibly discuss my capability to use DEET as a mosquito repellent, my capability to protect myself against mosquito bites, my capability to remain free from malaria, or my capability to be healthy. Not only may a certain level of capability analysis make more sense depending on the problem at hand, it may also be that we do not discern something as a moral problem unless we look at capabilities at a certain level of abstraction. Take another example not discussed by Briggle, namely the mobile phone. At a micro level of analysis, an individual is continuously able to make a lot of choices – about whether to make a certain call with his cell phone, call this or that person, make the call later or not at all, or use texting instead, and so on. At a somewhat higher level of analysis, the one which pluralist theorists of technology prefer, the person may be seen to be free to use his phone for maintaining friendships in this way or another, to use the phone as part of certain business practices or not, or even to discard her cell phone completely. Yet if we zoom out even further and look at the person from a bird's-eye view, it may be very hard – at least in the West, but increasingly also elsewhere – to decide to lead a life that does not include mobile telecommunication and being reachable by others most of the time. Patterns that develop at a larger scale may mean that you are sometimes forced into certain functionings, like being reachable for your boss even during the holidays. It may also mean that you lose valuable human capabilities when you get rid of your phone, like being able to find and hold onto all sorts of jobs. Likewise, Briggle remarks that it has serious consequences if you are the only person without e-mail or voice mail. Often collective action will be needed – or at least very helpful – to try and change such patterns again, if we judge that this negatively affects our well-being and freedom. In Germany for example several companies and the ministry of labour have introduced guidelines and technical measures in an attempt to 'free' employees from the pressure to read e-mail after hours.[12]

Multiple realizability of capabilities and the capability–functioning distinction

At this point it may be useful to briefly summarize what has been discussed so far. The first section of the chapter made clear that individual human capabilities are actually thoroughly social by nature. Groups, social practices, institutions, social structures and the like are crucial constitutive parts of people's capabilities. It was next discussed that technical artefacts not only can be given a place in this contextual and relational ontology of the capability approach, but that indeed it is necessary to put technical artefacts in this perspective. The effect of technical artefacts on human capabilities depends on how exactly they are embedded in broader socio-technical networks. At the same time technical artefacts partly shape such networks. Thus it is not only important to zoom in on the details of design, as was argued in the previous section, but also to zoom out to see the broader picture. If we want to introduce new technical artefacts in order to expand human capabilities, for example in the context of development projects, it is necessary to also invest in the surrounding socio-technical networks. This requires understanding the complexity of the network rather than a piecemeal focus on separate conversion factors. The second part of the chapter explored the question whether the 'network character' of technology has any serious implications for the possibility of individuals attaining the real and effective freedom to realize the life they have reason to value. The answer to this question, so it was argued, depends on how strong and pervasive one takes the network character of technology to be. Based on a paper by Briggle (2009) a distinction was made between two broad and general views, namely the pluralist and the system view of technology – with the latter raising more concerns about the freedom of the individual to realize his own particular view of the good life.

The remaining pressing question on the reader's mind may now very well be: so which view is closer to the reality on the ground? The pluralist or the system view of technology? Posed in this way, this question is impossible to answer for a number of reasons. First, these two views have been sketched in a broad and general way. Under each of these views one could think of various more specific accounts of what technology is, how it functions, how it relates to the good life, how it co-shapes society and so on. It is these more specific accounts, rather than the general view, which need to be judged on their merits. Second, as was discussed before, it is partly a matter of choosing at which level of abstraction to analyse things – a choice which may partly be influenced by moral considerations, such as which capabilities at which level of abstraction deserve ethical scrutiny. Third, ever since the empirical turn in philosophy of technology there is widespread agreement that it is necessary to look at concrete technologies in concrete contexts of implementation, rather than sustaining talk about 'technology' in general (Kroes and Meijers 2000). There is very little that you can say about the influence of technology on valuable human freedoms in general terms. The modest aim of the second part of this chapter has been to challenge simplistic views about technology as a neutral instrument that merely expands valuable human capabilities without imposing a specific sort of life on anyone. When investigating concrete cases one will most likely find that some technologies have very strong system effects, whereas others are more 'localized' and compatible with many other technologies and a variety of usage practices. In both cases reflection on technology and the good life is desirable, but in the cases of the first kind the need for public deliberation is more urgent and the ethical dilemmas may be bigger.

The capability approach could provide a conceptual framework for such assessments and evaluations of technology. For example, we could use Nussbaum's list of ten categories of centrally important capabilities to discuss the implications of certain socio-technical arrangements for our effective freedom to lead a life we have reason to value. A question that arises though is to what degree this list itself is neutral towards different views of the good life. It is a topic of debate whether or not Nussbaum's version of the capability approach itself fits with liberalism[13] and leaves people sufficient freedom to realize their own ideal of the good life, as she claims, or whether it is paternalistic as it imposes a specific view of the good life on people (Barclay 2003; Deneulin 2002). As Sen has never made such a capability list, he has not received such fierce criticism for imposing a specific view of the good life. However, Deneulin (2002) has argued that actual policies based on Sen's version will be more paternalist than his theory admits, as unavoidably choices need to be made about which capabilities to promote.[14] Even if policy makers come to a different list based on participatory public deliberation, there will most likely still be people who disagree. Deneulin finds Nussbaum's version of the capability approach 'more sincere' (p. 498) in the sense that it is explicit about the issue. The responses that Nussbaum (2000: 105 and 2006: 78–80) has given to the charges against her list include (1) drawing attention to the 'multiple realizability' of the capabilities on her list and (2) to re-emphasize the importance of the 'capability–functioning distinction' (see the Introduction). The effectiveness of these responses has been questioned by Nussbaum's opponents, but it is beyond the scope of this book to go into the details of this debate. Of course Nussbaum never intended to address the concerns about technology, individual freedom and the good life. However it is interesting to explore whether her two points can do so. What will be argued in the remainder of this section is that the ideas of the 'capability–functioning distinction' and 'multiple realizability' seem especially compelling if one adopts the pluralist view of technology. However, they will most likely not take away the concerns about individual freedom and neutrality towards the good life of somebody who adopts a strong system view of technology.

One of Nussbaum's responses to her opponents is that her list of ten central capabilities is still quite abstract and allows for 'multiple realizability:

each of the capabilities may be concretely realized in a variety of different ways, in accordance with individual tastes, local circumstances, and traditions' (Nussbaum 2000: 105). Thus, to give an example, in Southern Africa and in Western Europe they will most likely have different understandings of the meaning of having a capability for 'affiliation' ('being able to live with and toward others', as Nussbaum describes it), and different ideas about how to guarantee that all people have it. However, it should be noted that within any region or country there will most likely also be diverging ideas of what it is to lead a good life, including how to live well with and toward others. This means that multiple realizability – or rather multiple *realization* – would also be a desirable feature at a more local level. Multiple realization would increase people's capability set not with more different capabilities,[15] but by bringing different ways to realize the same capability within people's reach. At this point it becomes interesting to return again to the distinction between pluralist views of technology and system views of technology. If a pluralist view of technology is the most convincing, we have the best prospects of realizing a general, abstract capability in multiple ways simultaneously. Respect for pluralism or people's different views of the good life then means stimulating the availability of a wide range of technologies and accompanying social practices, without it being necessary to make any hard choices on the best technology or way of living. If a system view of technology is most convincing, we will tend to be more pessimistic about this possibility. Take Facebook. You may disagree with its implicit view of what it means to 'live well with and towards others'. It may not match your view of the good life. Yet if all your friends and acquaintances centre their social life around Facebook, your individual freedom to choose an alternative way of engaging with them is constrained. Moreover, it will also not be so easy to successfully start an alternative type of social network site that integrates another interpretation of living well with and towards others in its design – as mass usage is exactly what makes Facebook a success.

Another response of Nussbaum to the critique that her list reflects a particular view of the good life has been to highlight the importance of the capability–functioning distinction that the capability approach makes. Public policies should, according to capability scholars, generally aim at merely expanding people's capabilities, but not force them into the corresponding functionings. So if certain functionings are not in line with a person's view of the good life, (s)he may chose not to realize it. Implementing Nussbaum's list could therefore – at least in theory – be done in a way that respects pluralism in what people value in life. Deneulin (2002), however, has forcefully argued that this distinction is – for several reasons – impossible to consistently maintain in policy practice. One reason is that there are a lot of interdependencies between all sorts of functionings and capabilities, both at the individual and the collective level. The previous chapter already mentioned these interdependencies at the individual level. For example, someone who has the capability to be healthy but makes life choices that seriously damage his health also jeopardizes many other capabilities.[16] Deneulin illustrates the interdependencies between functionings and capabilities at a collective level with Nussbaum's capability for 'play', another one of the ten items on her list. Nussbaum describes it as 'being able to laugh, to play, to enjoy recreational activities' (Nussbaum 2000: 80). In her work Nussbaum, says Deneulin, regularly gives the example that a person with opportunities for play and leisure should be left free to choose a workaholic life. Since employers have a preference for people that work more rather than less, Deneulin fears however that in the long term everyone will be less and less free to take leisure time – unless government enforces compulsory legal holidays, which comes down to forcing people into not choosing the functioning 'work' during these days. Interestingly, this particular example resembles the example of e-mail and mobile phones making it harder and harder for people enjoying undisturbed free time – unless collective measures are taken to protect people against such intrusions. Humans live in societies that lead to an increase in their capabilities, which cannot be created without any interdependencies between people embedded in social practices and structures. Technology, especially when understood as having strong system-level effects, should be taken as aggravating such interdependencies. An implication of the system view of technology is arguably that it is hard if not impossible to always maintain the capability–functioning distinction in practice, useful as the distinction may be in our deliberations. Yet if the pluralist view of technology is overall more plausible, the capability–functioning distinction can be maintained more easily. The technical artefact in question may not be neutral towards the good life, it may contain a specific interpretation of valuable capabilities, but as long as it does not force anyone into certain functionings there does – in the pluralist view on technology – not seem to be a real problem.

To conclude: in the capability approach freedom is not, as Kullman and Lee (2012: 44) argue, a matter of 'liberation from' the context in which people find themselves. It is rather a matter of 'liberation within' this context, by reshaping the social and material interdependencies which both enable and constrain people. The capability approach is neither able to change the fundamental nature of technology, nor the fundamental nature of our social reality. It is thus not able to solve at a fundamental level the challenges that these pose. It cannot take away the need to deliberate about technological developments, social change and the good life. As Van den Hoven (2012) has argued, we have to let go of any idea of complete public neutrality towards the good life that is unfeasible and unworkable in our technological age – that is, if we do not want to forego the many benefits that technology brings in terms of well-being and our ability to realize the good life. We will then collectively have to evaluate and assess technologies in those terms. For this purpose the capability approach can provide a vocabulary and valuable ideas.

Notes

1   The first part of this chapter is based on Oosterlaken (2011), the second part on Oosterlaken (2013: ch. 7).
2   Note that this 'practical' criticism is different from a normative criticism which has been voiced against the capability approach, namely that it reflects a particularly Western normative perspective, whereas in many developing countries more value is attached to the community and collective goals. There are various ways in which one could defend the capability approach against this criticism, and Sen and Nussbaum have both addressed it extensively in their work.
3   An informative collection of short papers on collectivity and the capability approach can be found in the June 2013 issue of *Maitreyee*, the e-bulletin of the Human Development & Capability Association. It can be downloaded at http://hd-ca.org/publications/maitreyee-june-2013-collectivity-in-the-ca (accessed 15 October 2014).
4   An example can be found in the following quote from Drèze and Sen (2002: 6): 'The word "social" in the expression "social opportunity"… is a useful reminder not to view individuals and their opportunities in isolated terms. The options that a person has depend greatly on relations with others and on what the state and other institutions do. We shall be particularly concerned with those opportunities that are strongly influenced by social circumstances and public policy.'
5   Following Martins (2006, 2007), Smith and Seward argue that Sen, in using concepts such as 'well-being', 'advantage' and 'capability', is operating on the level of scientific ontology. Both Martins and Smith and Seward (2009) are instead concerned with the more abstract level of philosophical ontology. The general philosophical ontology that the latter adopt as most compatible with Sen's writings is critical realism. It is beyond the scope of this book to discuss the details of this view, or how it compares to other philosophical ontologies.
6   Moreover, on the level of philosophical ontology his account seems very compatible with that of Smith and Seward, as both are based on a critical realist ontology. For a further reflection on critical realism and the capability approach, see Oosterlaken (2013: ch. 5, annex).

7   Philosophers of technology are likely to associate the phrase 'expanding human capabilities' (used in the capability approach literature) with 'extension theory' within their field, which Lawson (2010: 208) describes as 'any theory in which technical objects are conceived of as some kind of extension of the human organism by way of replicating, amplifying, or supplementing bodily or mental faculties or capabilities'. This idea of extending human capabilities is clearly different from the idea of expanding human capabilities put forward in the literature on the capability approach. Lawson explicitly distinguishes this type of extension theory from his own idea of the sense in which technology extends human capabilities. And his own proposal comes rather close to the concept as it is being used within the capability approach.

8   There are interesting parallels that one could draw between the body of thought of Sen as founder of the capability approach on the one side, and Latour as founder of ANT on the other side (Kullman and Lee 2012). Yet it should also be noted that the concept of 'agency', which is very central in both ANT and in the capability approach, is not understood or used in the same way by both thinkers. Autonomous human intentions are key to Sen's understanding of agency, whereas Latour's concept of agency is by and large mechanistic. In short, certain insights from ANT are certainly useful if one wishes to give technology a place in the capability approach, but one needs to be aware that one should sometimes explicitly drop or selectively accept certain parts of either view to ensure coherence (Oosterlaken, 2013).

9   In a way this is of course true. Searle (2010: 17/18) makes the useful distinction here between epistemological and ontological objectivity. Ontology is about what exists, epistemology is about what we can know about those things which exist. Social institutions are subjective in the ontological sense, in the sense that they only exist because people acknowledge their existence and 'play their part' in upholding them. However, our knowledge about these institutions, Searle argues, is epistemologically objective. We can for example establish whether it is true or not that there is a nation state called Canada, or that dollar bills can be used to make payments in the USA. This truth is a matter of fact, not opinion.

10 Note though that Sen himself also discusses the notion of conversion *functions* in some of his work. A function formally describes the relation between different entities. The argument made here, so Martin van Hees has pointed out to me, does not seem to apply to these conversion functions. However, as much work on the capability approach does make casual references to all sorts of different conversion factors rather than such functions it seems still useful to invite the reader to critically reflect on this notion.

11 This 'and so on' is important, because even an apparently simple socio-technical network in which a simple technical artefact is embedded can – on further analysis – turn out to consist of many elements (see the case of mp3 players in Chapter 4).

12 See www.telegraph.co.uk/news/worldnews/europe/germany/10276815/Out-of-hours-working-banned-by-German-labour-ministry.html

13 As philosophical debates on liberalism are very complicated, it is beyond the scope of this book to further discuss this issue.

14 On Sen, liberalism and neutrality, see also Lowry (2009).
15 At least not on Nussbaum's level of abstraction. However, whether something is a different capability or a variety of the same capability seems to depend on which level of abstraction one adopts.
16 As was mentioned in the previous chapter, some technologies are explicitly designed to be behaviour-steering – in other words, these technologies are meant to promote certain human functionings or even force people into these functionings. Yet if people are aware of this behaviour-steering aspect and fully free to choose to use the technology or not, this is not in tension with the capability–functioning distinction. People may for example choose the technology if their considered judgement is that the behaviour is desirable, but weakness of will threatens to undermine their ability to follow up on this choice.

References

Barclay, L. (2003). What Kind of Liberal Is Martha Nussbaum? *SATS – Nordic Journal of Philosophy* 4(2).
Briggle, A. (2009). Technology, the good life, and liberalism: some reflections on two principles of neutrality. Paper presented at the 16th Biennial Conference of the Society for Philosophy and Technology (SPT 2009: Converging Technologies, Changing Societies). University of Twente, Enschede, the Netherlands.
Deneulin, S. (2002). Perfectionism, Paternalism and Liberalism in Sen and Nussbaum's Capability Approach. *Review of Political Economy* 14(4):497–518.
Drèze, J. and Sen, A. (2002). *India: Development and Participation*. Oxford: Oxford University Press.
Geels, F.W. (2004). Understanding System Innovations: A Critical Literature Review and a Conceptual Synthesis. In: Elzen, B., Geels, F.W. and Green, K. (2004). *System Innovation and the Transition to Sustainability: Theory, Evidence and Policy*. Cheltenham: Edward Elgar.
Ibrahim, S. (2006). From Individual to Collective Capabilities: The Capability Approach as a Conceptual Framework for Self-help. *Journal of Human Development* 7(3):397–416.
Kroes, P. and Meijers, A. (eds) (2000). *The Empirical Turn in the Philosophy of Technology*. Amsterdam: JAI/Elsevier.
Kullman, K. and Lee, N. (2012). Liberation from/Liberation within: Examining One Laptop per Child with Amartya Sen and Bruno Latour. In: Oosterlaken, I. and Van den Hoven, J. (eds), *The Capability Approach, Technology & Design*. Dordrecht: Springer.
Lawson, C. (2010). Technology and the Extension of Human Capabilities. *Journal for the Theory of Social Behaviour* 40(2):207–23.
Leydens, J.A., Lucena, J.A. and Nieusma, D. (2014). What is design for social justice? Paper presented at the 121st ASEE Annual Conference & Exposition, Indianapolis, IN, 15–18 June.
Lowry, C.R. (2009). Beyond Equality of What: Sen and Neutrality. *Les Ateliers de l'Éthique* 4(2): 226–35.

Martins, N. (2006). Capabilities as Causal Powers. *Cambridge Journal of Economics* 30:671–85.

Martins, N. (2007). Ethics, Ontology and Capabilities. *Review of Political Economy* 19(1):37–53.

Meerhof (2013). Pomphouders tegen Oplaadstations. In: *De Volkskrant*, 12 July (www.volkskrant.nl/dossier-archief/pomphouders-tegen-oplaadstations~a3474460, accessed 16 October 2014).

Mink, A., Parmar, V.S. and Kandachar, P.V. (2014). Responsible Design and Product Innovation from a Capability Perspective. In: Van den Hoven, J., Doorn, N., Swierstra, T., Koops, B.-J. and Romijn, H. (eds), *Responsible Innovation Volume 1: Innovative Solutions for Global Issues*. Dordrecht: Springer.

Nussbaum, M.C. (2000). *Women and Human Development; The Capability Approach*. New York: Cambridge University Press.

Nussbaum, M.C. (2006). *Frontiers of Justice; Disability, Nationality, Species Membership*. Cambridge, MA: Belknap Press of Harvard University Press.

Oosterlaken, I. (2011). Inserting Technology in the Relational Ontology of Sen's Capability Approach. *Journal of Human Development and Capabilities* 12(3):425–32.

Oosterlaken, I. (2013). Taking a capability approach to technology and its design – a philosophical exploration (doctoral dissertation), vol. 8. Simon Stevin Series in the Ethics of Technology (edited by Brey, Philip; Kroes, Peter; Meijers, Anthonie). 3TU.Centre for Ethics and Technology, Delft.

Radder, H. (2009). Why Technologies Are Inherently Normative. In: Meijers, A. (ed.), *Handbook of the Philosophy of Technology and Engineering Sciences*. Amsterdam: Reed Elsevier, pp. 887–922.

Robeyns, I. (2005). The Capability Approach – A Theoretical Survey. *Journal of Human Development* 6(1):94–114.

Searle, J. (2010). *Making the Social World; The Structure of Human Civilization*. Oxford: Oxford University Press.

Smith, M.L. and Seward, C. (2009). The Relational Ontology of Amartya Sen's Capability Approach: Incorporating Social and Individual Causes. *Journal of Human Development and Capabilities* 10(2):213–35.

Stewart, F. (2005). Groups and Capabilities. *Journal of Human Development* 6(2):185–204.

Van den Hoven, J. (2012). Neutrality and Technology: Ortega Y Gasset on the Good Life. In: Brey, P., Briggle, A. and Spence, E. (eds), *The Good Life in a Technological Age*. Abingdon, Oxon.: Routledge.

Winner, L. (1980). Do Artifacts Have Politics? *Daedalus* 109(1):121–36.

Wyatt, S. (2008). Technological Determinism Is Dead; Long Live Technological Determinism. In: Hacket, E.J., Amsterdamska, O., Lynch, M. and Wajcman, J. (eds), *The Handbook of Science and Technology Studies*. Cambridge, MA: MIT Press, pp. 165–80.

Zheng, Y. and Stahl, B.C. (2011). Technology, Capabilities and Critical Perspectives: What Can Critical Theory Contribute to Sen's Capability Approach? *Ethics and Information Technology* 13(2):69–80.

Zheng, Y. and Stahl, B.C. (2012). Evaluating Emerging ICTs: A Critical Capability Approach of Technology. In: Oosterlaken, I. and Van den Hoven, J. (eds), *The Capability Approach, Technology and Design*. Dordrecht: Springer.

4
A CAPABILITY APPROACH OF ICT FOR DEVELOPMENT (ICT4D)

Is there something special about ICT?

In the past two decades or so information and communication technologies (ICTs) have become immensely popular in development cooperation (Unwin 2009), getting this image of being powerful 'weapons against poverty'. A quite well-known example, because of regular attention in popular media, is that of mobile phones increasing the income of small-scale farmers in Africa, as the phones give them access to crop prices and enable them to circumvent middlemen.[1] In a brief article, titled 'The Mobile and the World', Amartya Sen (2010) also expressed his enthusiasm for the role that mobile phones can play in development. He points out that all technologies can, of course, in principle be used for good or for bad – like a gun for protecting innocent lives and a mobile phone for planning a terrorist attack. Yet, Sen claims (p. 1):

> A telephone owned by a person helps others to call the person up, as well as to receive calls from him or her, and so the increased freedom of the phone owner adds to the freedom of others. In contrast, a gun owned by one can easily reduce the freedom of others, if the gun is pointed at them – or could be. Many goods have little impact on others, as a shirt owned by one does not, typically, have much of an impact on the lives of others.

Thus contrary to other goods and technologies, Sen concludes, a phone 'is generally freedom-enhancing, and that is an appropriate enough point of departure for the hagiography of the mobile phone'. Without denying that mobile phones and other ICTs can make – and indeed already have made – a tremendous contribution to development and poverty reduction (see e.g. UNDP 2012), one may wonder whether the term 'hagiography' is not somewhat ill-chosen. It gives the mobile phone a saintly status, implicitly suggesting that ICT for Development (ICT4D) projects introducing or using this 'magic bullet' technology are beyond reproach. Sen has however repeatedly questioned the tendency to uncritically put another all-purpose means – income[2] – at the centre of development policy and evaluations. Technological change needs, just like economic growth, to be assessed in terms of ultimate societal goals, like enabling each and every person to lead a flourishing human life. ICTs are no exception to this – they are mere means, not ends in themselves.

The ICT4D 'hype' that arose at some point in development policy and practice has been followed by an increasing scholarly interest in the topic of ICT4D. Nowadays several specialized academic ICT4D journals exist. Despite all this research prominent ICT4D scholars have made calls to dig deeper. One of the conclusions of Walsham and Sahay (2006) in their overview of information systems research in developing countries, for example, is that there is not sufficient attention for the *meaning* of development and how ICTs promote or hinder meaningful development. Heeks (2010) states that when it comes to ICT4D research what is lacking is 'more theory-based evidence about ICTs' impact on development; especially for more evidence founded in theories that have currency within development studies' (p. 635). The capability approach could play a role here, as a perspective on the meaning of development which can be fruitfully connected to a range of explanatory theories. In the past years several ICT4D scholars have started to apply the capability approach in their research. In fact, an overwhelming majority of the available studies on 'technology and the capability approach' actually concerns ICT4D (Oosterlaken 2012). One can only speculate why ICT4D is so dominantly present in this literature. It can probably partly be explained by the fact that the capability approach has become especially influential in development studies, although the approach could equally well be applied to the global North – including the normative evaluation of emerging ICTs in this context (see e.g. Zheng and Stahl 2012). Part of the explanation may furthermore be that any development hype at a certain moment seems to give rise to a critical counter movement. And as will be discussed in more detail in the next section, ICT4D scholars have found a useful framework in the capability approach for voicing their criticism.

However, might it be a part of the explanation that there is something special about ICTs, as opposed to other technologies, after all? Something which makes the capability approach and ICT4D research/practice a potentially fruitful and interesting combination? As Kleine (2011) has pointed out, technologies such as mobile phones and the internet have – contrary to other technologies – a quite indeterminate character, in the sense that they give access to a wide range of information and communication opportunities. They can thus contribute to the expansion of human capabilities in very different areas: health, education, recreation, livelihoods, democracy, etc. Such ICTs might thus be seen as the ultimate embodiment of the ideal of the capability approach that we ought to promote a variety of capabilities and leave it up to empowered individuals to choose which functionings to realize through their usage of the ICT, depending on their idea about the good life. Of course many ICTs are designed to serve a specific function and are not that open to a variety of usages, and design may further influence or limit the choices that people (can) make. Still, the internet and mobile phones in general may be seen to have this open character. As the internet is by nature a multifunctional technology allowing for a lot of choice, Kleine (2011) argues, it 'is particularly well-suited to be a test-case for the [freedom and] choice paradigm [that the capability approach offers] in development evaluation, execution and planning' (p. 120). In practices this sometimes gives rise to ethical dilemmas, as will be discussed later in this chapter. More specifically, there may sometimes be a tension between the values of well-being and agency.

On further reflection: Sen is also not wrong about the immense importance of mobile phones – or the internet for that matter – connecting people. The previous chapter extensively discussed that from an ethical perspective *individual* capabilities may be important, but that by nature such capabilities are actually *social* through and through. The existence of individual capabilities depends heavily on how individuals are embedded in social structures and in groups. ICTs like the internet and mobile phones have of course made possible completely new ways of forming groups and communities, and have strongly reshaped existing social structures. In addition, Foster and Handy (2008) argue, it is very important what personal relationships a person can maintain. They introduce the term 'external capabilities'[3] for those capabilities that a person acquires as a result of being directly connected to another person. It is thus a specific sub-class of capabilities, one in which the personal relationship with another person is a key component. An illiterate person, so they pose by way of example, may increase her capabilities by developing a good personal relationship with a literate person. And a farmer who becomes friends with somebody with an internet connection gains the external capability of access to crop prices. ICTs not only expand individual capabilities, Foster and Handy conclude, ICTs also 'makes them easier to share as external capabilities' (p. 369). At the same time, so these authors acknowledge, the quality and security of such 'proximate capabilities' may not be the same as capabilities created in other ways.

To conclude this section: there might indeed be something special about ICT which makes it worthwhile to discuss in some more detail. A more practical consideration to devote a chapter in this book to ICT4D is that there is plenty of material available in this domain which can illustrate the different ways in which the capability approach can be applied to technology, and its benefits and limitations. This chapter will make good use of these existing scholarly studies on the capability approach and ICT4D.[4] The vast amount of literature that is now available makes it impossible to be complete and exhaustive[5] – and to attempt to do so would be pointless anyway, as newly appearing studies would soon date such an overview. Rather, the point of this chapter, and this book as a whole, is to increase the reader's understanding of the capability approach in relation to technology. In a way ICT4D is, like the appropriate technology (AT) movement discussed in Chapter 1, another case that contributes to that goal. The next section will discuss various ways in which 'mainstream' ICT4D has been criticized from the perspective of the capability approach. Following that, the third section of this chapter will discuss a case study, namely a project of Practical Action in which mp3 players and podcasts were introduced in a rural area in Zimbabwe. One of the attractive features of this case is that it illustrates the 'zooming in–zooming out' perspective which was presented in the Introduction, and which structured Chapters 2 and 3. The fourth section will then pay special attention to the values of well-being and agency in development, and the tension that may arise between both in ICT4D practice. This will be done on the basis of the podcasting case and that of the telecentres. The last section of this chapter discusses the various ways in which the capability approach could be operationalized within ICT4D, with the aim of further illustrating the versatility of the approach.

Criticisms of capability scholars on 'mainstream' ICT4D

Several scholars have in the past decade made a general plea for applying the capability approach to ICT4D, because they felt unsatisfied with 'mainstream' ICT4D practice and scholarship (e.g. Alampay 2006; James 2006; Kleine 2011; Zheng 2009 – see Oosterlaken 2012 for an extensive inventory of the literature). Of course the field of ICT4D is nowadays huge, and quite diverse. These criticisms will therefore certainly not apply to all the work that is being done in this area. One may even wonder if there is such a thing as a unified 'mainstream' ICT4D field, or how this could be distinguished from 'alternative' ICT4D research and practice. This chapter will not address those questions, as it is in a sense not primarily about ICT4D – but about the capability approach, and what perspective it has to offer on ICT4D. The reader who is familiar with certain work in the area of ICT4D should decide for her or himself whether a particular criticism applies to that, and whether the capability approach has something of value to offer for that particular type of work. Not surprisingly, the lines of criticism that capability scholars have voiced on 'mainstream' ICT4D have a clear overlap with the issues discussed in Chapter 1 relative to technology more broadly. In line with the main concepts and themes in the capability approach literature, this section will discuss the interconnected topics of (a) the means–ends distinction and the multidimensionality of well-being, (b) human diversity, conversion factors and distributive justice and (c) agency, aspirations and choice.

One criticism of mainstream ICT4D practice has been that there is too much emphasis on the contribution of ICTs to economic growth. This focus has been said to be 'too narrow to capture the impacts of ICT' (Kleine 2010: 675). Economic growth will of course lead to an increase in the available means, and this is important. However, the capability approach warns us not to confuse means and ends. One of the ultimate ends of development projects, according to the capability approach, should be an increase in people's well-being – understood in terms of valuable functionings and capabilities. ICTs may contribute to well-being indirectly, through economic improvements, but ICTs may often also contribute to well-being in a more direct way. As Kleine (2010: 683) puts it:

> ICT and development practitioners work with multi-purpose technologies which offer far more significant changes to people's lives than the economic impact they might have. Moving away from an a priori, top-down and often overly economistic set of development, priorities

offers the chance to recognise the diversity of the contributions ICTs can make to the social, cultural, environmental and economic aspirations individuals may have for their lives.

In the capability approach well-being is considered to be multidimensional: it is a matter of the person having a range of capabilities in different domains of life, so that (s)he can live the life that (s)he has reason to value. In her recent book Kleine (2013) gives many examples of how ICTs may have an impact on people's lives. One type of ICT intervention that she extensively discusses is that of the telecentres or publicly funded internet cafes that have – before the mobile phone hype – been introduced in many rural areas in developing countries in order to give people access to the internet and other ICT services at low cost or free of charge. These telecentres may have economic benefits to people. In addition, Kleine claims:

> knowing that the people who one cares about are safe and happy, understanding more about one's history and identity, imagining travel to faraway places, talking to people from other cultures, knowing what is going on in the world as well as national and local politics, expressing a view online, or simply enjoying music or testing one's skill in games are all elements of the lives people may value.
>
> *(p. 125)*[6]

Such a view of well-being being multidimensional also allows for a more nuanced analysis of the impacts of ICT4D projects, which may reveal both positive and negative impacts on people's well-being. Even mobile phones may sometimes have negative impacts. Based on two surveys among income-poor households in Kenya, Nyambura Ndung'u and Waema (2011) give various examples of negative impacts that people perceive in the areas of crime, privacy–security, anxiety–stress and social relations. Interestingly, but perhaps not surprisingly, these problems seem very similar to those that people in the global North sometimes face. For example, some people reported the problem that employers now expect them to be reachable and answer calls on any moment of the day, all week. The total body of evidence that is by now available on mobile phones seems to support the claim that overall they have tremendous positive capability impacts, which by far outweigh the negative impacts (Smith *et al.* 2010). However, we sometimes need to look beyond aggregates to reveal – and subsequently address – specific issues. Generally, Heeks (2014) concludes after an extensive literature review, in ICT4D there is little attention for the costs, failures, disbenefits or negative impacts of ICT – the dominant view being that 'ICT is a wonderful thing and our challenge is to help everyone have effective access' (p. 12). Proposing to broaden impact assessments beyond economic benefits and defending the multidimensionality of well-being of course does not imply that every ICT4D project should target the full range of valuable capabilities and functionings. It also still leaves open the question which capabilities and functionings matter, and how to decide this. These are questions which are extensively discussed in the capability approach literature, and the last section briefly takes them up.

A second line of criticism has been that there is too much attention focused on merely giving people access to ICTs (Alampay 2006), even though the impact or 'outcome is contingent, depending on individual conversion factors' (James 2006: 339). Measuring development success in terms of resource distribution and (formal) access is only a proxy for the real impact on people's lives, and we sometimes have to look beyond measurements that aggregate over different individuals. When we look at the level of specific individuals, sectors or regions it may for example become visible that due to different conversion factors, the introduction of mobile phones will lead to different outcomes in terms of capability expansion for different (categories of) individuals (Wahid and Furuholt 2012). An example that James (2006) discusses is that of the internet, and the 'telecentres' in which people can access the internet. He refers to studies that indicate that factors such as literacy, age and socio-economic status influence not only whether people are truly able to access or use the internet at all in these communal facilities, but also whether individuals are enabled to realize new valuable functions as a result of internet usage. One conversion factor that Kleine (2013) highlights in her discussion of telecentres is gender. The usage of time and space, she argues, is subject to gender norms. Because of this women may be less able to derive benefits from the mere existence of telecentres than men. In her Chilean case she finds that restrictions on time indeed make it harder for women to benefit. On the other hand the telecentres are sometimes more beneficial for women, as they have so few other spaces where they can legitimately assemble. Another conversion factor that she identifies as highly relevant is a person's income. While she praises the free access telecentre models linked to libraries, she notes that in some telecentre models the centres do raise user charges, particularly once the donor funding ends. As a result, in such instances conflicts may arise, Kleine claims, between the goals of including marginalized groups and being financially sustainable as a result of revenues through service charges. The implementation of new ICTs may thus, Kleine concludes, raise concerns of distributive justice. These concerns may be partly conceptualized in terms of differences between people in the conversion factors that apply to them and in the differences in resulting individual capability sets. Another example can be found in an article by Thomas and Parayil (2008), who – also based on the capability approach – gathered some empirical evidence in India that ICTs may sometimes increase inequality, because the socially advantaged classes tend to be more able to convert access to ICT into something useful in their lives than those that are deprived. Sen's basic observation that the presence of resources does not always lead to capability expansion for each and every person applies thus just as much to ICTs as to other technologies. Such insights may offer points of departure for further policies, projects or initiatives for change.

Chapter 1 of this book presented the AT movement as a locus of experience in dealing with 'conversion factors' through design solutions. Somewhat surprisingly, the ideas of the AT movement do not seem to have taken much hold in the field of ICT4D (Van Reijswoud 2009). Chapter 2 discussed the idea of 'capability sensitive design', a variation on the idea of 'value sensitive design' (VSD) – a design movement which has its roots in the field of human–computer interaction. Yet, to date, design and the values implicated in design, does not seem to get much attention in the ICT4D literature (Johri and Pal 2012). It is furthermore noteworthy that ICTs might be considered special not only in terms of the potential discussed in the previous section, but also in terms of giving rise to an extra challenge. A challenge that arises from the fact that actually two different resources are involved here: the technological artefact and the information distributed or made accessible. Therefore, ICTs, one could perhaps say, seem to face a 'double conversion challenge'. Different personal, social or environmental factors may apply to both the technology and the information. To expand people's capabilities it is for example not enough to make sure that people have the skills to use an ICT application, we also need to ensure that they have the skills to make good use of the information accessed in this way. According to Talyarkhan *et al.* (2005), ICT4D projects

> connecting the first mile often assume that improved access to ICTs leads to improved access to information, which leads to improved knowledge and decision making and therefore development outcomes. Evidence from projects suggests that in many cases the information is

difficult to appropriate because it is exogenous, in an inaccessible format, or not from a source people trust.

(p. 18)

A nice example can be found in Rhodes (2009), who quotes from an interview with the manager of an African telecentre which was meant to be helpful to local entrepreneurs:

> We tried, and everywhere we went, at meetings and conferences people told us how good the Internet is, how we can find customers, we felt very stupid because we know people are using the Internet to help them with business, but we could not do it. We know we can do market research with the Internet, but how can we do this, we cannot understand how.
>
> (p. 13)

Here it is not so much the technical artefact, but the information itself that invokes conversion problems. To bring about the envisioned expansion of capabilities it may therefore be crucial to pay attention to the appropriateness of both the technological resource and the informational resource made accessible. An alternative or complementary strategy – depending on the case – may of course be to pay attention to people's skills to understand, process and use the information that is available. From the quote above it is not clear whether the information available on the internet is not useful in the local circumstances, or whether the skills of local people are insufficient to convert the information into valuable capabilities, or a combination of both.

A third line of criticism is that 'users and potential users of ICT are often perceived as passive receivers of innovations, as many technologies are transferred to "developing" countries from contexts of more advanced economies, and are often imposed on local users under the claim that these particular technologies are "good for them"' (Zheng 2009: 77). The capability approach – or at least in its broad usage,[7] as was discussed extensively in Chapter 1 – considers agency to be a central value in development. Respecting or promoting agency implies, says Zheng, that inclusive participation and public deliberation need to be part of the process of implementing ICTs. It also implies giving voice to people in the process of technology choice and/or design preceding adoption, and the process of evaluation following diffusion. Especially in 'the context of multi-purpose technologies [like ICTs] which could empower individuals to attain development outcomes of their own choosing', Kleine (2010: 675) claims, 'the common way of measuring impact by defining the intended development outcomes top-down and a-priori is unsuitable'. The question was raised before how to decide about which capabilities/functionings matter when evaluating development impacts, and many capability scholars hold that participatory methods have a crucial role to play (Crocker 2008; Frediani 2007). This does not mean that development evaluation is limited to uncritical acceptance of the desires that people express, or the preferences that they display in their behaviour. The capability approach acknowledges that preferences may sometimes be distorted by situations of extreme poverty and deprivation. In addition, it has been argued that exclusively relying on existing preferences may be especially problematic when it comes to new technologies, as prospective users may not have the knowledge and experience to make judgements about the value of a technology for their lives (Johnstone 2007). Both problems are however no reason to abstain from participatory methods, but rather to think carefully about how to best implement them. A perhaps more fundamental challenge is noted by Kleine (2011), who asserts that the funders on which development organizations depend are generally not inclined to commit resources based on the promise that a project will empower people to make their own choices. Rather, they are interested in more predictable, predetermined project goals.

So is this criticism of 'mainstream' ICT4D new, or are these criticisms that can only be made in terms of the vocabulary of the capability approach? The answer to both questions should be no. As Zheng (2007: 8) observed, 'many issues unveiled by applying the capability approach are not new to e-development' or ICT4D. However the capability approach has, she says, the potential to 'surface a set of key concerns systematically and coherently, on an explicit philosophical foundation'. In order to illustrate the sort of concerns that the capability approach would highlight, the next section discusses an ICT4D project from the perspective of the capability approach. This ICT4D project was briefly mentioned in Chapter 1, and this section will discuss it more extensively.[8] The project does not seem representative of 'mainstream' ICT4D practice, in the sense that it is firmly rooted in the appropriate technology movement.[9] The case is interesting to discuss in this chapter, because it can be taken to illustrate various points:

- the lens that the capability approach offers on ICT4D projects;
- the usefulness of both 'zooming in' on the details of design and 'zooming out' to the socio-technical embedding of artefacts (see Figure 4.1); and

- the need to reflect on both well-being and agency (to be discussed in the next section).

However, the fact that only this case is discussed in detail in this chapter should not be taken as an implicit claim that this type of project is to be preferred from the perspective of the capability approach. As was argued extensively in Chapter 1, the capability approach as such still allows for a wide range of views on how technology can best be made to contribute to human development.

A case: mp3 players in Zimbabwe

'Kamuchina kemombe' is the name that local people in the Mbire district, Lower Guruve area in Zimbabwe, have given to the mp3 players that have been introduced in the area. The literal translation of this is 'a machine with knowledge of cattle management' (Grimshaw and Gudza 2010). The simple reason for this name is that most of the podcasts made available along with the mp3 players contained lessons on cattle management, although also some podcasts on health care issues were recorded. Both the mp3 players and the podcasts were introduced in 2007 by the British development organization Practical Action and its local partner organization LGDA. The introduction of this technology was part of the pilot project Local Content, Local Voice, which builds on earlier work within Practical Action on the question of how to 'connect the first mile' – how to deal with the challenge of 'sharing information with people who have little experience of ICTs, low levels of literacy, little time or money, and highly contextualized knowledge and language requirements' (Talyarkhan et al. 2005: xi). Such challenges also apply to the Lower Guruve area. Literacy, for example, is 75 per cent (Grimshaw and Gudza, 2010: 6). In many other respects as well the development challenges are big in this semi-arid area: livelihoods are mainly dependent on small-scale subsistence farming (livestock production and drought resistant crop cultivation); and the district's infrastructure services in the district are poor (no electricity, running water, telephone landline, mobile phone network or FM radio network). Traditional agricultural extension services, which are meant to distribute relevant agricultural information, had ceased to be reliable because of poor transport and other economic reasons. One of the bottlenecks was, for example, that governmental livestock officers did not have enough time to properly train animators interacting with the villagers. The mp3 players were introduced as an additional channel for knowledge

114 A capability approach of ICT4D

sharing rather than a replacement. Local animators were trained and provided with the mp3 players, on which podcasts were played during group meetings or upon request from individuals. Hence the process of sharing knowledge came to be regarded as 'digital extension'.

Taking a capability approach to this case would first and foremost mean recognizing that a successful development project is not a matter of merely giving access to resources like mp3 players. What are people now as a result able to do and be, which they could not do and be before? The current project evaluation reports limit themselves largely to outcomes in terms of the number of podcasts recorded and distributed, the decrease in animal mortality, the increased milk yields from the animals and increased crop productivity (Mika 2009: 9). Of course strengthening people's livelihoods means strengthening their ability to support themselves. If successful, it would imply increasing people's basic capabilities, their 'freedom to do some basic things that are necessary for survival and to escape poverty' (Robeyns 2005: 101). As capabilities can be both an end in themselves as well as a means for the expansion of other capabilities, this may – in a positive spiral – also contribute to the expansion of further capabilities. One farmer for example mentioned that he was now able to pay school fees for his children as a result of his increased number of cattle and increased crop yields. As a result, these children may acquire more capabilities. Yet there may be other, less tangible project impacts. According to another local farmer the mp3 players fostered group work and group harmony, something which was previously missing. When groups ask for podcast lessons, he reported, they share experiences and ideas. So according to this farmer the technology improved farmers' relations with each other and with the development

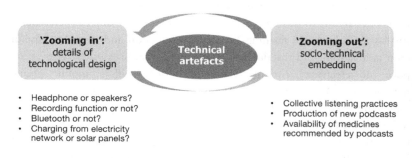

Figure 4.1 The 'zooming in–zooming out' movement applied to the case

agents. The project also seems to give farmers more self-esteem, or a sense of identity and agency, as expressed by yet another farmer when asked about the project's benefits: 'before the technology, if an animal was dying then I could not take action, but now I can. I am happy since I am a full farmer now!' (Janssen 2010: 70–1). If one attaches importance to both well-being and agency, such impacts are certainly worth taking into consideration. In short, the capability approach could provide a conceptual framework for a more comprehensive evaluation of the project.

Furthermore, the capability approach would draw attention to the conversion factors that influence whether certain technical artefacts lead to the expansion of valuable capabilities in certain circumstances or for certain categories of people. Often gender differences are significant, and that also applied to this case. For example, during group meetings men were seated close to the (mostly male) animator and the mp3 player. Sometimes their speaking volume was impossible to hear for the women who were sitting approximately 10 meters back. Men were also more actively involved in the discussion after the broadcast. Women sometimes needed to ask their husbands permission to visit the animator individually to hear a podcast (Janssen 2010: 72). Such factors may, however subtle, influence the conversion of a technology into valuable human capabilities. From a capability perspective gender-related differences in conversion factors seem to deserve a more detailed investigation, but unfortunately they did not receive much explicit attention during the project. Chapter 1 discussed some possible responses to the gender issue raised by this case. Sometimes conversion factors may be effectively taken into account in the design of a technology, or by choosing a technology with suitable characteristics or design features. In the Local Content, Local Voice project, for example, it was investigated whether solar energy panels to charge the batteries of the mp3 players would be an appropriate response to the lack of an electricity grid in the area. In the end, a choice was made for taking the mp3 players back to the LDGA office, outside the area and in reach of an electricity grid, for recharging.[10] It was furthermore acknowledged early on that the impact of ICT may be different for literate and illiterate people. By opting for a voice-based rather than a text-based technology it was ensured that both groups would benefit. The project also acknowledged that there is a 'double conversion challenge', in the sense that conversion factors may apply to both the technical artefact and the information made accessible. Information is also a resource that does not always convert in valuable outcomes, and this needs to be explicitly addressed. The information needs of the local population were thoroughly investigated at the beginning of the project. The podcasts were created in the local language and with the least educated farmers in the community in mind, so that the information would be understandable for everybody (Grimshaw and Gudza 2010).

In Chapter 3 it was argued that technical artefacts generally only expand human capabilities when they are properly embedded in broader sociotechnical systems. In the case of the Local Content, Local Voice project as well, it is not merely the podcasting device that expands human capabilities. Rather, as Janssen (2010) describes, an extensive actor network had to be created around these devices (see Figure 4.2). The old network in which information dissemination took place was quite simple, the elements being notebooks, pencils, livestock officers, animators, community members and group representatives. That the podcasting devices were able to expand human capabilities as compared to the old situation was due to a new and more extensive network. This network includes – among others – the podcasting devices, the loudspeakers, the laptop with the database with podcast, the batteries, the charger at the head office of LGDA, the car to transport the batteries, the electricity grid available there (which was lacking in the pilot area), the different government departments involved in providing the contents of the podcasts, employees of LGDA and Practical Action and the person with the right local dialect who is able to record clear podcasts. And the exact composition of and relations within the network turned out to matter for the expansion of human capabilities. For example, the new and expensive cattle treatments recommended by the podcasts, such as vaccinations, were not always available or affordable for all the farmers. This was a limiting factor for the impact of the podcasts on human capabilities. In other words: the local network lacked medicines and actors making them available to local people. Partly as a result of this, local people requested that indigenous knowledge be captured in podcasts as well. This was done (without verifying this knowledge in any scientific way). Recording practices thus matter for the outcome. Furthermore, certain practices had to be developed within the network after the introduction of the devices. For example, it became clear during the project that villagers sometimes still had difficulties putting the information of the podcasts to use. This was solved by starting to organize additional demonstration meetings, showing – for example – how to treat sick cattle in the way explained by the podcasts. The case study can also illustrate that it is important how a specific individual is positioned vis-à-vis the network as a whole. Obviously, people depending on livestock and crops for their livelihoods gained the most capabilities as a

A capability approach of ICT4D **117**

result of the introduction of the mp3 players. On the other hand the basic capabilities of some traditional healers seemed to diminish due to the podcasting devices, as they more or less lost clientele to the device, people that would previously have gone to these healers with their health issues or sick cattle. The livestock animators benefited the most, since they closely related to the mp3 players and had access to its knowledge all the time. People who lived close to the animator went more often to him to demand individual lessons (Janssen 2010).

Finally, from the perspective of the capability approach one should also look at the *process* that led to the achieved development impacts. The Local Content, Local Voice project was part of a larger EC block grant project with the objective to improve livestock health and product value of resource poor households in the Mbire District. In the preparation phase, local people made a prioritization of possible interventions within the scope of this project. Also at later stages opportunities for participation were present. A wide range of stakeholders, including agricultural and veterinary agencies, local government, local development associations, community workers and local village chiefs

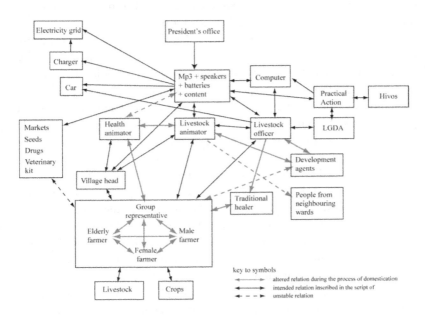

Figure 4.2 Network surrounding mp3 players in April–July 2010 (source: Janssen 2010)

were involved in the process. Participation was also built into the process of the sub-project Local Content, Local Voice. The process by which people acquired knowledge, via agricultural extension, were mapped and key stakeholders included in all the dialogues. People were also consulted on the proposed technical solution. This led to design changes, such as the addition of loudspeakers to the device in order to enable collective listening while sitting under a tree in the village. Thus, a way of information sharing was made possible that is very much in line with local cultural practices. According to Practical Action the participatory process has been an important factor in bringing about a high degree of technology uptake. However, in the view of the capability approach, participation should not just be considered to be of instrumental importance to goals such as technology adoption. Participation in collective deliberation and decision-making is first and foremost seen as being important for normative reasons; it is respectful of human agency to put people in the driver's seat of projects that try to improve their lives. To determine to which degree this is the case Crocker (2008), for example, presents a classification of modes of increasing participation. This classification could be used to provide a detailed analysis of the degree of participation in small-scale development projects. Such analysis could reveal that there is room for improvement, but has not been undertaken for this case.

To conclude: although Local Content, Local Voice was never explicitly conceptualized, implemented or evaluated by Practical Action in terms of the capability approach, the project thus seems – on the face of it – to be doing quite all right from this perspective. A full evaluation in line with the capability approach would take into account the multidimensionality of poverty and well-being, the degree of local participation and the possible differences in development impacts between categories of individuals. The next section will pay some extra attention to well-being and agency as two central values in the capability approach literature. Often agency and well-being may go hand in hand, and even mutually strengthen each other in a beneficial, upward cycle of development. However, often there will be clashes and then questions may arise about which of the two values to prioritize in a certain context or at a certain point in the development process. This will be discussed in more detail on the basis of two cases – one being the podcasting project in Zimbabwe, the other being the case of telecentres and community radio. In the former the issue of well-being versus agency arose in the phase of technology choice, in the latter it arose in the implementation or usage phase. Both cases highlight interesting yet different aspects and dimensions of the issue of 'well-being versus agency'.

Agency versus well-being as goals for ICT4D projects

Let us start with the case of telecentres, alluded to earlier. People may use their access to the internet for many different purposes. Many of these purposes could in principle be recognized as valuable within a multidimensional account of well-being such as the capability approach. What was also briefly discussed is Kleine's (2011) claim that open-ended technologies like the mobile phone and the internet are in principle an ideal test case for a development paradigm like the capability approach, which aims to empower people to realize the life they have reason to value. Yet, she notes, the donors who drive the formulation, implementation and evaluation of development projects generally have a preference for clearly defined development outcomes instead. An insightful discussion of this very issue can be found in an unconnected[11] article by Ratan and Bailur (2007). They refer to a range of studies that show that there is often a gap between how telecentres are actually used and the intentions that development organizations had for the project. What donors and NGOs aim at, they note, is a 'well-being usage' of telecentres, a usage which contributes to quite uncontroversial development goals in areas such as health, nutrition, education and agricultural yield. What often happens in practice is that people use the computers for entertainment – playing games, chatting, accessing videos and music, or viewing pornography (when content blockers do not filter this out). This phenomenon is of course not limited to internet access through telecentres alone. Kivunuke et al. (2011) held a survey and groups discussions in Uganda to determine the relation that people perceive between their quality of life and various ICTs promoted by the Ugandan Rural Communications Development Fund (RCDF). They also conclude (p. 75) that 'the preferred uses of ICT under the prevailing circumstances were entertainment and keeping in touch with family and friends rather than the frequently promoted aspects regarding people's well-being such as education, etc.'.

The ethical dilemma that arises, Ratan and Bailur notice, is whether NGOs should respect such usages out of respect for people's agency, or whether it is acceptable to respond in a paternalistic way. They illustrate this dilemma with a case study that they did in an Indian village, of a project called Our Voices which combined a telecentre and community radio. The radio part of the project was supposed to make information available on topics which were considered relevant, such as on crops, market prices and women's health. An interesting passage from their case findings is the following:

We were told by villagers that the radio set medium had been phased out soon after implementation (one of the reasons given was that the villagers started taking the radios out to their field and listened to FM radio instead of Our Voices). During research, some listeners dismantled one of the radio loudspeakers in protest and used it to accompany the procession of the statue for a religious festival. The NGO's reaction to this was that the people were ignorant and uninterested in their own 'development'. They removed all the cabling, and set up the loudspeaker in another village.

(p. 124)

Now on the surface it may seem simple which answer the capability approach would suggest to the ethical dilemma of how the NGO should respond to the entertainment usage of the radios – respect people's agency. In reality it is not so obvious. For example, the capability approach acknowledges the existence of severely distorted or adaptive preferences. The value of agency therefore does not imply that each and every expression of a person's unreflected preferences always needs to be respected. Yet surely, one may respond, we should save the label 'adaptive' for preferences which have been formed in situations of severe oppression or poverty, otherwise respect for agency does not have any bite. Let us assume for argument's sake that there is no occurrence of such adaptive preferences here.[12] We could then next point out that there is no reason to exclude the usages mentioned from the list of valuable development outcomes. Nussbaum, for example, includes 'affiliation'[13] and 'play' on her list of ten central categories of valuable human capabilities – so exactly matching the preferred usages mentioned by Kivunike et al. (2011). Nussbaum also defends the view that the capabilities on her list are all incommensurable components of a flourishing human life. Since the actual ICT usages also contribute to some aspect of well-being, what argument could the NGO have to withdraw support? In response to this question, one might point out that Nussbaum holds that justice requires bringing people *up to a threshold level* of each of the ten capability categories on her list. This puts arguably moral obligations on us as global citizens, which we discharge of through the work of organizations like this NGO. However, once people are over the threshold level for a minimum decent life for a certain capability, there may not be a moral obligation to support further expansion. Depending on where we put the threshold and on the facts of the case, one might therefore be able to argue that the NGO is not morally obliged to support using ICTs for entertainment purposes, contrary to health and education usages. In short, the capability approach can play a role in our moral deliberations, but often does not provide simple and straightforward answers. Careful ethical deliberation is needed in such cases.

The contribution that Ratan and Bailur (2007) themselves make to ethical reasoning about their case is twofold. First, they notice that the NGO as the provider of Our Voices assumes that local people have some form of bounded rationality, and that the NGO knows better what is good for them. 'But what about the bounded rationality of the provider?,' Ratan and Bailur (p. 126) ask. How certain are we that NGOs have a realistic estimation of the well-being improvements made possible by the ICT in question? NGOs are after all often 'outsiders' and therefore have restricted knowledge of local conditions. Ratan and Bailur elaborate:

> In an environment where healthcare centres almost always lack good doctors and medication, what is the use of identifying that one's baby has dysentery using a healthcare information system? In an environment where there are limited opportunities for those with a Bachelor's degree in Arts from a rural government college, what is the use of listing oneself in an online job search application? The analogies to other 'welfare' ICT[4]D applications are apparent. There are severe constraints in the translation of information into desired welfare outcomes in most developing country contexts today, given poor infrastructure, dismal public service provision, weak governance and rigid labour markets.
>
> (p. 127)

In short: due to a range of conversion or structural factors information does not necessarily lead to an expansion of capabilities. Thus the choice that people seem to make for an entertainment usage of the available ICTs may be an indicator of the absence of the intended capability expansion, rather than a genuine choice between different feasible functionings. Second, Ratan and Bailur point out that the well-being benefits of entertainment usages of the ICTs are immediate – they lead to happiness or at least fewer worries for some time. The well-being benefits that the NGO wishes to promote, however, are benefits which tend to materialize more in the long term, if at all – even if the time investment in ICT usage is made now. A rational ICT usage decision is therefore also a matter of how to discount future benefits. Ratan and Bailur refer to economic work by Banjeree and Duflo (2006) to argue that 'these significant trade-offs between valuations of the present and the future are indeed exacerbated among low-income families, given the context of high uncertainty in which they live from day to day' (p. 128). To conclude, it is not so obvious what the choice is that a rational, fully informed person would or should make.

Let us move on to the podcasting project in Zimbabwe. In their discussion of the rationale behind the project, Practical Action employees Grimshaw and Gudza (2010) argue that both media type and content source should be acknowledged as determinants of changes in the unequal global balance of power – as a consequence of which digital exclusion is still a problem. They argue that text based media as made available through the internet tends to tip the balance of power away from local people. They propose that this is the reverse 'if voice media and local content are used', as was done in this project:

> Empowering rural communities with information and knowledge can upset the social and political status quo. For example, communities become aware of their national entitlements to farming inputs such as seed, fertilisers, livestock drugs and availability of drugs at their local clinics. Local government agents become inundated with enquiries and demands for which they have to do something about. We worked with the communities to understand their development challenges and any solutions we found, including technical solutions, which resulted from these consultations, became communities' solutions and not our own.
>
> *(p. 9)*

Assuming that communities are never homogeneous, but actually comprise people with different interests and power, a question which arises is what makes a solution truly a 'community solution' – or how this is decided. Unfortunately the article does not provide further details. The question ties in with issues which were already raised in Chapter 1, namely the challenge that power differences pose for participatory methods, and the claim that it is an advantage of appropriate technology that generally 'it is less disruptive to the [existing] social structure' (Hazeltine and Bull 1999: 6). The latter increases the chances of a successful adoption of the new technology, and is therefore a factor to take into consideration. Yet sometimes a disruption of existing social structures is needed to increase the well-being of certain categories of individuals to empower them. Grimshaw and Gudza (2010: 9) claim that in the Local Content, Local Voice project stakeholders were well aware that technology has the potential to challenge and even change the power relations in a community. Ratan and Bailur (2007: 127) mention an incident in the Our Voices project where 'residents asked where public funds went when a local government (panchayat) meeting was broadcast, and subsequently the panchayat refused to have further relations with *Our Voices*'. In short, the dilemma that sometimes arises is that of choosing between contributing to the transformation of the existing social structures, or choosing the technology that is most appropriate to the current situation and therefore most likely to be successfully adopted (Smith *et al.* 2014: 114).

It may be fruitful to conceptualize the dilemma at hand as prioritizing an increase in the well-being of marginalized groups in the short term, versus prioritizing the more risky possibility of increasing agency and justice in the long term. More concretely, this dilemma manifested itself in relation to investigations by Practical Action – in an early phase of the project – into the possibility to integrate Bluetooth technology in the technical solution that would be implemented. The usage of Bluetooth technology would enable the easy exchange of podcasts between devices that are in each other's vicinity. The original idea was furthermore that not only selected animators, but people at large would get direct access to the mp3 players, and would be able to record their own podcasts. In the end, simple mp3 players without Bluetooth were implemented. Several factors seem to have contributed to this. The final project report by Practical Action mentions political interference as one of the threats that the project faced (Mika 2009), without specifying details. An interview by Janssen (2010) with the responsible team leader of the local partner organization of Practical Action reveals that there was a fear that the devices would be used to disseminate critical political messages about Mugabe's regime. The security agents from the President's office would, so it was estimated, hold the development organization responsible if this were to happen. However, technical and financial problems also played a role in the decision and are the official explanation for not implementing Bluetooth after all. Further research would be necessary to disentangle the exact role of different causal factors and actors in the technology choice made. What is certain is that the recording function that allowed the livestock officers to create new lessons was disabled before giving the mp3 players to the local animators. This means that new podcasts could only be added at the NGO office. Podcasts were originally produced and distributed on a limited number of topics only, in the domains of health and cattle management. Villagers did have influence on the contents, as participatory methods were used early in the project to determine their development priorities and information needs. Once the project was running, they could also make requests for new podcasting topics to the animators. Yet, on the face of it, this arrangement seems to limit the agency and capability expansion of individuals in comparison with other ICT alternatives. One such alternative is the one which was investigated and tested early in the project, where people would be able to directly record their own knowledge and questions, which could then – with the help of Bluetooth technology – be disseminated throughout the network of device owners. Another alternative that one might want to consider is that of a telecentre.

We could place these three alternative technologies on the 'determinism continuum' (Figure 4.3) proposed by Kleine (2011: 120), which indicates how strongly a technology determines how people use it. Generally, Kleine claims, 'the further down on the determinism continuum a specific technology is, the more danger there is that the technology circumscribes the choices of a user-citizen more than that it widens them', or – put differently – the more danger there is that the technology is not judged positively from the perspective of the capability approach (unless design decisions reducing choice would have been made with the users themselves). Telecentres would go a long way towards the 'open-ended' extreme of the continuum and of the three alternatives mentioned, the restrained podcasting devices introduced by the project would be most towards the 'closed' side of the continuum. Kleine's concept of a 'determinism continuum' may be a useful analytical tool, but it needs to be applied without excessive focus on merely the technology in isolation from the context in which it is to be implemented – otherwise there is a risk of invoking exactly the mistake that the capability approach attempts to avoid, namely an excessive focus on the resources or technologies themselves, overlooking what people can actually do or be because of them. The question whether or not human capabilities are being expanded is very much a matter of 'all things considered'. In the context of the Lower Guruve area in Zimbabwe, telecentres – despite their being open-ended in principle – would in reality not contribute anything to the expansion of human capabilities of the people living there, considering conversion factors like the absence of electricity in the villages at the time. Even in places where the existing 'conversion factors' are not so clearly fatal, there may be more subtle factors at play that mean the telecentres do not live up to the expectations (Ratan and Bailur 2007).

In the Local Content, Local Voice project, however, great care has been taken to ensure that the podcasts are understandable to the local people and directly applicable in their everyday life. The first evaluation results indicate that it has led to people reaping a higher income from their livestock and

A capability approach of ICT4D **125**

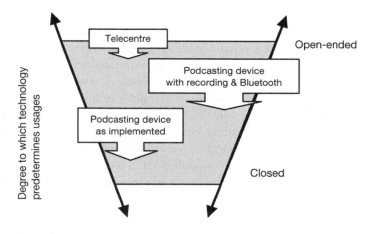

Figure 4.3 Positioning technological alternatives on Kleine's (2011) determinism continuum

improved health, which can be expected to contribute in turn to expanding people's capabilities to lead the lives they have reason to value. Something similar might be argued for podcasting devices with a recording function and Bluetooth technology; this technology is more open-ended in principle. As compared to the technological alternative actually introduced in the Mbire area, it has the potential to contribute more to the agency of local people, as this alternative would allow them to record and disseminate their own knowledge and messages, without having to depend on the willingness of some employee of an NGO to grant a request to address a certain topic in a new podcast. However, in reality these potential agency benefits may never have been fully realized, not only because of technical and financial constraints, but also considering the pending pressure of the President's office to intervene in the work of the NGO and the distribution of the devices in case of unwelcome recordings. The devices that have actually been introduced by Practical Action may not be optimal from the agency perspective, but they may arguably be better from the well-being perspective, as they seem to contribute in a sustainable way to the enhancement of local livelihoods and thus to the expansion of a range of capabilities and so-called 'functionings'.

Still, it remains a dilemma. Around the world, ICTs have also proved their value as tools in changing unjust and corrupt regimes, being a force of change that these regimes have found hard to control. Should an NGO aim for expanding agency in the long term, knowing the risk that a project upsets the local power balance too much and therefore fails or gets shut down? Or should its emphasis be on achieving much less uncertain well-being goals? In the Local Content, Local Voice case this becomes a choice between two different technical alternatives. Which one would have been better remains a question open for further debate – which would need to take into account not only normative considerations, but also practical and strategic considerations. Kleine argues that for more closed technology applications the litmus test should be whether the choices embedded in the technology align with the choices of the end users. To achieve this, Kleine argues that there should be user participation in the decision-making process: 'the more users' choices will later be locked in by the technology, the more the users' choices must already be integrated in the design process' (Kleine 2011: 126). Participation is thus central if we want to respect people's agency, also in the process of engineering design and technological choice. Note though that this may make the 'scaling up' of a solution which has been developed and tested in a project more problematic, as the new context of application may differ substantially from the context of origin of a technology.

To conclude, the two cases illustrate each in their own way that agency and well-being goals may point in different directions, which poses a dilemma that the capability approach may help to conceptualize – although the capability approach alone will not suggest a straightforward solution. The case discussed by Ratan and Bailur (2007) shows that such dilemmas may arise after implementation, in the usage of technology. The second case reveals that such dilemmas may already exist in the phase of engineering design or technology choice.

The versatility of the capability approach

The past sections have explained the relevance and potential of the capability approach for the field of ICT4D, and have further illustrated this by means of some cases. This section will discuss a selected number of other publications on the capability approach and ICT4D, with the aim of further illustrating the versatility of the approach and discussing some issues which deserve further attention.

One of these issues is that the capability approach as a general conceptual framework will often need to be supplemented with additional theories that help us understand certain aspects of ICT4D. And some of the insights offered by the capability approach may resemble insights which already exist in certain strands of ICT4D literature. Zheng (2007) gives a range of examples (p. 10) of potentially relevant additional and/or compatible perspectives. The literature on the so-called 'digital divide', she notes, is just like the capability approach 'concerned with effective opportunities for people to exploit ICTs'. And the literature on the topic of information infrastructure is, according to her, relevant when we ask the question which conversion factors often determine whether or not an ICT will lead to actual capability expansion. A related issue for the capability approach as a general conceptual framework is that there is not one single way to 'operationalize' it. Operationalization 'needs to occur ... at many different levels, and in respect to different problems' (Alkire 2005: 127). Even for the specific challenge of evaluating the local development impact of certain ICTs or ICT4D initiatives there is not one obviously best way to do this – as one can conclude when comparing the methodologies of some of the studies so far (e.g. Gigler 2008; Grunfeld, Hak, and Pin 2011; Kivunike et al. 2011; Madon 2004; Vaughan 2011; Wahid and Furuholt 2012; Zheng and Walsham 2008). Zheng and Walsham (2008), for example, consider the capability deprivations of and capability impacts for different types of actors or stakeholders in their cases. Gigler (2008) and Vaughan (2011) look not only to individual capability expansions, but also to the expansion of collective capabilities. Differences of course also occur with respect to the question of which capabilities to take into account, and how to determine this. For example, Kivunike et al. (2011) use a wide range of literature in order to arrive at a list of potential ICT opportunities in different domains, which is then applied to their case. Vaughan (2011) on the other hand takes a more participatory, bottom-up approach to arrive at a list of capabilities to which ICTs have contributed in her case. Generally, differences in how the capability approach is operationalized in ICT4D research will partly be due to different disciplinary backgrounds and theoretical commitments of researchers.

So far the most elaborate effort to put the capability approach to use in ICT4D research has been made by Dorothea Kleine. She has developed her so-called 'choice framework' (Figure 4.4) in a range of publications and applied to a number of cases (Kleine 2010, 2011, 2013; Kleine et al. 2012). She considers the conceptual richness of the capability approach, and therefore the difficulty of operationalizing it, to be the main reason why it has not really caught on in development practice. Her work takes some important steps towards making the capability approach understandable and usable for policy makers and practitioners in ICT4D. Kleine's choice framework is heavily inspired by the capability approach, but also draws on other theoretical resources. It draws on Giddens's (1984) structuration theory, which assumes a reciprocal relationship between social structure and individual agency. This is a theoretical commitment which is by and large in keeping with the discussion on the relational nature of individual capabilities as presented in Chapter 3. It should be noted though that Kleine's interpretation of the term 'agency' deviates from how it is generally used in the capability approach (see Introduction). She considers the magnitude of an individual's agency to be 'measured by an individual's asset endowment' or 'resource' portfolio (p. 42) rather than a result of the interaction between individual and social structure.[14] Actual technical artefacts appear as 'material resources' in a person's resource portfolio. In addition she conceptualizes ICTs as having structural aspects that people have to navigate in order to realize the life they have reason to value, while also affecting the relative worth of the other individual resources in their portfolios. An example that she gives in her recent book (Kleine, 2013) is that of the government e-procurement system Chilecompra, introduced in Chile in 2005. This forced entrepreneurs to acquire contracts in an entirely new way, and the demands posed by the system turned out to be especially difficult to meet for micro- and small-scale businesses. Hence it tended to affect the capabilities of these business owners negatively. As compared to the old situation, Kleine (p. 182) concludes, the system furthermore 'devalued social resources (bids were anonymized) while increasing the role of material resources (means of production ... that could help companies achieve economies of scale to win a price competition)'. Kleine's choice framework (Figure 4.4) suggests collecting data on changes to both (the extent of) people's resource portfolios and to social structures, and investigating their interactions.[15] Furthermore it incorporates the empowerment framework of Alsop and Heinsohn (2005), which distinguishes between the existence, use and achievement of choice. To this Kleine adds 'sense of choice', as she finds this especially important in the case of new technologies, which offer possibilities that people may be unaware of.

When applying the capability approach to ICT4D, it can be used for different purposes and on different levels. Kleine (2011: 125–6), for example, sees three types of application for which her choice framework may be useful, namely (1) for 'deconstructing embedded ideologies' in certain ICTs, (2) to 'map the complex influence ICTs have on development processes', and (3) for 'proactive' planning of ICT4D projects and programs. Much work on the capability approach and ICT4D so far has been focused on the second

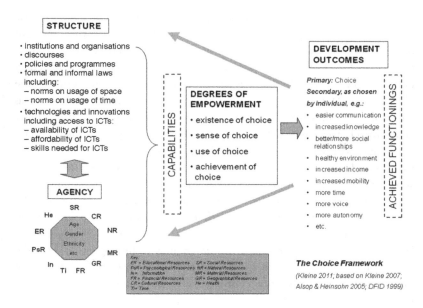

Figure 4.4 The choice framework developed by Kleine (2013)

application. This actually consists of two parts. There is an evaluative part, which is core to the capability approach literature more broadly, namely assessing – in terms of capabilities and functionings – the well-being of certain groups, the outcomes of small-scale development projects, the overall development level of countries, and so on (Robeyns 2006). And there is a descriptive part, in which researchers try to map the factors that causally contribute to these 'objects' of assessment. Such research leads to knowledge that may be used for what Alkire (2008) has called 'prospective applications' of the capability approach. This concerns recommendations on which of the available courses of actions contributes most to the expansion of valuable capabilities, which is needed for the third application that Kleine mentions for her choice framework – proactive planning of ICT4D projects and programs. Of course Kleine's framework provides just one way to map the relation between ICTs and the expansion of capabilities and functionings. It is important to critically discuss any such operationalization, as what one sees through the lens of the capability approach will partly depend on which 'filters' – such as accounts of technology – one adds as a supplement to the capability approach.

Regarding the first mentioned application of the choice framework, deconstructing embedded ideologies, Kleine emphasizes that it is important to consider how much choice ICTs leave to people. The fewer choices a technology leaves open to people, she argues, the more important it generally becomes to consider which values have been incorporated into it during the design phase. Her case study of the Chilecompra system can again serve as an example. Kleine shows that the design of this system – determining collective choices on which goods and services to buy – assumed certain values and goals to be central to development (such as increasing competitiveness and cost efficiency) and was at the expense of others (for example achieving distributive justice through regional economic development, or sustainability). However, in the end we do not just want to deconstruct the values embedded in existing ICTs – although this definitely needs to happen if one considers transferring a technology to a new context of application. What is also necessary is to proactively design new technologies – or redesign existing technologies – so that they will embed our best understandings of the relevant values in a specific context of application. It seems therefore that Kleine's list of types of application may benefit from an explicit formulation of a fourth application. Just as the second exercise (mapping causal relations) can be coupled to the third application (proactive planning), it seems that the first application (deconstructing embedded values) can and should be coupled to proactively designing for values. This idea was extensively discussed in Chapter 2, although not in any way specific for ICT4D.[16] It is likely that Kleine assumed this to be part and parcel of proactive planning for ICT4D projects and programs. It seems useful though to make this more explicit, as to date design does not seem to get much attention in the ICT4D literature (Johri and Pal 2012). Also the ideas of the AT movement, to which design was crucial, do not seem to have taken much hold in the field of ICT4D (Van Reijswoud 2009).

Although measuring capabilities is in various ways challenging (Comim 2008) and more difficult than for example measuring access to resources, progress has been made over the years in developing measurements (see e.g. Anand *et al.* 2009). Furthermore, both qualitative and quantitative applications of the capability approach exist at all levels of analysis – micro, meso and macro. Many of the existing studies applying the capability approach to ICT4D are investigating specific ICTs or ICT4D initiatives, often in a qualitative way. One example of a possible different type of ICT4D application can be found in a chapter by Barja and Gigler (2007). Inspired by the capability approach, they explore what sort of information could be used to assess 'information and communication poverty' at a regional level. Another example of a different type of application can be found in a contribution by Wresch (2007). He uses the capability approach to reflect on social justice concerns raised by the fact that the activities of website development and hosting are divided very unequally over countries in the world.

To conclude: the capability approach is a versatile approach that could be applied to ICT4D in various ways and at various levels. However, its implications for ICT4D have not yet been sufficiently explored in all possible directions. On the one hand this chapter was written with the modest goal of introducing the interested reader to the capability approach and its relevance for and application to ICT4D, drawing on some key studies that have already appeared on the topic but without the pretention of presenting a complete overview of the literature. On the other hand this chapter has tried to make a substantive contribution to the research on ICT4D and the capability approach by arguing for the importance of two things. The first is to pay attention to not only the socio-technical embedding of the technology in question, but also to the details of the design of the technical artefact. In addition, attention was drawn to the 'double conversion challenge' that ICT4D poses, in the sense that there are two types of resources involved – technical artefacts and information – which do not automatically lead to an expansion of capabilities. The second thing that this chapter has highlighted is the importance of explicitly addressing possible tensions between the values of agency and well-being that may arise in ICT4D practice.

Notes

1   See e.g. 'Five Ways Cell Phones Are Changing Agriculture in Africa,' http://foodtank.com/news/2013/04/five-ways-cell-phones-are-changing-agriculture-in-africa, or Seven Ways Mobile Phones Have Changed Lives in Africa http://edition.cnn.com/2012/09/13/world/africa/mobile-phones-change-africa (both accessed 22 May 2014).

2   In a way money possessed by one person may also, like the mobile phone, simultaneously contribute to the freedom of more people; when I spend a part of my income, other people generally gain income, such as for example the owner of the store where I spend my money. And the same happens when they in turn spend their money. This is known in economics as the multiplier effect of extra income. Of course, a difference with the mobile phone is that mere ownership of money by me is not enough to have an effect on the freedom of others.

3   As almost all capabilities are external in the sense explicated in Chapter 3, the term is perhaps not specific enough. The term 'relational capabilities' may

132 A capability approach of ICT4D

provide a better alternative, although that has the problem of already having other meanings and connotations. 'Proximate capabilities' is another alternative term worth considering.

4   For a reflection of an ICT4D practitioner on the capability approach, see Harmsen (2012).
5   The most complete and exhaustive overview to date can be found in Oosterlaken (2012).
6   This observation is not specific to ICT, but applies to development interventions more generally. Alkire (2002) for example discusses three case studies of income generation activities by Oxfam, and concludes that 'the activities' tangible income, and their associated effects on life, health and economic security were never regarded as the *most* important impacts by participants (p. 234). One of the cases concerns a rose cultivation project, in which the roses were processed into garlands used in local religious practices. Alkire finds that the women participating in the project highly appreciated impacts such as improved social relations between participants, having creative and aesthetically pleasing work, and being able to contribute to a valued religious practice.
7   See the last section of Chapter 1 for a discussion of the place and understanding of agency in the capability approach.
8   This case study was previously published as a book chapter (Oosterlaken *et al.* 2012). The main sources of information for the case study are documentation of Practical Action about the project, its predecessors and the ideas behind the project (Gudza 2009; Mika 2009; Talyarkhan *et al.* 2005), fieldwork by Pim Janssen in the period April–August 2010 (Janssen 2010) and experiences of David Grimshaw with the case and its predecessors while working for Practical Action (reflected upon in Grimshaw and Ara 2007; Grimshaw and Gudza 2010).
9   The AT movement as a whole got an image of being concerned only with simple, primitive solutions, such as a smoke hood or gravity ropeway. mp3 players are a more recent invention, but of course also not the most advanced form of ICT. Yet it is not per definition the case that modern, advanced technologies cannot also be AT (Grimshaw 2004).
10 These days there are however technological solutions for some such problems, see for example wwww.brck.com
11 'Unconnected' in the sense that Kleine does not refer to it in her recent work on the same topic (2010, 2011, 2013).
12 Of course there is more that could be said about this issue. For example, there is the challenge that the capability approach, as was already discussed in Chapter 1, does not contain a specific theory of preference formation. Moreover we do not have a lot of details on the case and relevant circumstances to base our judgements on.
13 With 'affiliation' she means among others the following: 'Being able to live with and towards others ... to engage in various forms of social interaction ... to have the capability for both justice and friendship' (Nussbaum 2000: 79).
14 When I recently had the opportunity to ask Kleine about this, she admitted that it was a dilemma: to narrowly follow conceptual conventions in the capability

approach literature on the one hand, or to present things in a way that would be accessible for her intended audience. She chose the latter.

15 For this purpose Kleine provides a list of ten types of individual resources (psychological resources, time, social capital, etc.), by drawing on and extending the idea of individual 'livelihood assets' (part of the well-known 'sustainable livelihoods framework'). A list of key structural elements is also part of the choice framework.

16 Note that the VSD approach has its roots in the field of human–computer interaction. VSD then became integrated in the field of computer ethics, before also being studied in ethics of technology more broadly (Van den Hoven 2007). It has so far hardly been applied in the context of developing countries.

References

Alampay, E. (2006). Beyond Access to ICTs: Measuring Capabilities in the Information Society. *International Journal of Education and Development Using Information and Communication Technology* 2(3):4–22.

Alkire, S. (2002). *Valuing Freedoms: Sen's Capability Approach and Poverty Reduction*. Oxford: Oxford University Press.

Alkire, S. (2005). Why the Capability Approach? *Journal of Human Development* 6(1):115–33.

Alkire, S. (2008). Using the Capability Approach: Prospective and Evaluative Analyses. In: Comim, F., Qizilbash, M. and Alkire, S. (eds), *The Capability Approach: Concepts, Measures and Applications*. Cambridge: Cambridge University Press.

Alsop, R. and Heinsohn, N. (2005). Measuring Empowerment in Practice: Structuring Analysis and Framing Indicators. In: World Bank, Washington, DC.

Anand, P., Hunter, G., Carter, I., Dowding, K., Guala, F. and Van Hees, M. (2009). The Development of Capability Indicators. *Journal of Human Development and Capabilities* 10(1):125–52.

Banjeree, A. and Duflo, E. (2006). The Economic Lives of the Poor. www.cid.harvard.eud/bread/papers/working/135.pdf

Barja, G. and Gigler, B.-S. (2007). The Concept of Information Poverty and How to Measure it in the Latin American Context. In: Galperin, H. and Marsical, J. (eds), *Digital Poverty: Perspectives from Latin America and the Caribbean*. Ottawa: IDRC.

Comim, F. (2008). Measuring Capabilities. In: Comim, F., Qizilbash, M. and Alkire, S. (eds), *The Capability Approach: Concepts, Measures and Applications*. Cambridge: Cambridge University Press.

Crocker, D.A. (2008). *Ethics of Global Development: Agency, Capability, and Deliberative Democracy*. Cambridge: Cambridge University Press.

Foster, J.E. and Handy, C. (2008). External Capabilities. In: Basu, K. and Kanbur, R. (eds), *Arguments for a Better World: Essays in Honor of Amartya Sen*. Oxford: Oxford University Press, pp. 362–74.

Frediani, A.A. (2007). Participatory Methods and the Capability Approach. In: *Briefing Notes*. Human Development and Capability Association.

Giddens, A. (1984). *The Constitution of Society*. Cambridge: Polity.

Gigler, B.-S. (2008). Enacting and Interpreting Technology – From Usage to Wellbeing: Experiences of Indigenous Peoples with ICTs. In: Van Slyke, C. (ed.), *Information Communication Technologies: Concepts, Methodologies, Tools, and Applications*. Hershey: IGI Global.

Grimshaw, D.J. (2004). The Intermediate Technology of the Information Age. In: *New Technologies Briefing Paper No. 1, June 2004*. Practical Action, Rugby.

Grimshaw, D.J., and Ara, R. (2007). Local Content in Local Voices. In: *ICT Update*. pp. 4–5.

Grimshaw, D.J., and Gudza, L.D. (2010). Local Voices Enhance Knowledge Uptake: Sharing Local Content in Local Voices. *Electronic Journal on Information Systems in Developing Countries* 40(3):1–12.

Grunfeld, H., Hak, S. and Pin, T. (2011). Understanding Benefits Realisation of iREACH from a Capability Approach Perspective. *Ethics and Information Technology* 13(2):151–72.

Gudza, L.D. (2009). Sharing local content in local voices; spreading the use of Podcasting – pilot project PODCASTING, End-of-Pilot Project Report submitted to HIVOS. In: Practical Action, Harare.

Harmsen, S. (2012). ICT for Human and Sector Development: Reflections from Practice. In: *Maitreyee, the e-bulletin of the Human Development and Capability Association*, March 2012 (theme issue on innovation, technology and design).

Hazeltine, B. and Bull, C. (1999). *Appropriate Technology: Tools, Choices, and Implications*. San Diego, CA/London: Academic Press.

Heeks, R. (2010). Do Information and Communication Technologies (ICTs) Contribute to Development? *Journal of International Development* 22:625–40.

Heeks, R. (2014). ICT4D 2016: New Priorities for ICT4D Policy, Practice and WSIS in a Post-2015 World. In: *Development Informatics Working Paper Series (paper no. 59)*. Centre for Development Informatics, Institute for Development Policy and Management, University of Manchester, Manchester.

James, J. (2006). The Internet and Poverty in Developing Countries: Welfare Economics versus a Functionings-based Approach. *Futures* 38(3):337–49.

Janssen, P. (2010). Kamuchina Kemombe: opening the black-box of technology within the capability approach. Master's thesis, University of Twente.

Johnstone, J. (2007). Technology as Empowerment: A Capability Approach to Computer Ethics. *Ethics and Information Technology* 9(1):73–87.

Johri, A. and Pal, J. (2012). Capable and Convivial Design (CCD): A Framework for Designing Information and Communication Technologies for Human Development. *Information Technology for Development* 18(1):61–75.

Kivunike, F.N., Ekenberg, L., Danielson, M. and Tusubira, F.F. (2011). Perceptions of the Role of ICT on Quality of Life in Rural Communities in Uganda. *Information Technology for Development* 17(1):61–80.

Kleine, D. (2010). ICT4What? – Using the Choice Framework to Operationalise the Capability Approach to Development. *Journal of International Development* 22(5):674–92.

Kleine, D. (2011). The Capability Approach and the 'Medium Of Choice': Steps towards Conceptualising Information and Communication Technologies for Development. *Ethics and Information Technology* 13(2):119–30.

Kleine, D. (2013). *Technologies of Choice?: ICTs, Development, and the Capabilities Approach*. Cambridge, MA: MIT Press.

Kleine, D., Light, A. and Montero, M.-J. (2012). Signifiers of the Life We Value? – Considering Human Development, Technologies and Fair Trade from the Perspective of the Capabilities Approach. *Information Technology for Development* 18(1):42–60.

Madon, S. (2004). Evaluating the Developmental Impact of E-governance Initiatives: An Exploratory Framework. *Electronic Journal of Information Systems in Developing Countries* 20(5):1–13.

Mika, L. (2009). Sharing local content in local voices; spreading the use of Podcasting pilot project – Final Evaluation Report. Practical Action Southern Africa, Harare.

Nussbaum, M.C. (2000). *Women and Human Development: The Capability Approach*. New York: Cambridge University Press.

Nyambura Ndung'u, M. and Waema, T.M. (2011). Development Outcomes of Internet and Mobile Phones Use in Kenya: The Households' Perspectives. *Info* 13(3):110–24.

Oosterlaken, I. (2012). The Capability Approach and Technology: Taking Stock and Looking Ahead. In: Oosterlaken, I. and Van den Hoven, J. (eds), *The Capability Approach, Technology and Design*. Dordrecht: Springer, pp. 3–26.

Oosterlaken, I., Grimshaw, D.J. and Janssen, P. (2012). Marrying the Capability Approach, Appropriate Technology and STS: The Case of Podcasting Devices in Zimbabwe. In: Oosterlaken, I. and Van den Hoven, J. (eds), *The Capability Approach, Technology and Design*. Dordrecht: Springer, pp. 113–33.

Ratan, A.L. and Bailur, S. (2007). Welfare, Agency and 'ICT for Development'. In: *ICTD 2007 – Proceedings of the 2nd IEEE/ACM International Conference on Information and Communication Technologies and Development*. IEEE, Bangalore, India.

Rhodes, J. (2009). Using Actor–Network Theory to Trace and ICT (Telecenter) Implementation Trajectory in an African Women's Micro-enterprise Development Organization. *Information Technologies and International Development* 5(3):1–20.

Robeyns, I. (2005). The Capability Approach – A Theoretical Survey. *Journal of Human Development* 6(1):94–114.

Robeyns, I. (2006). The Capability Approach in Practice. *Journal of Political Philosophy* 14(3):351–76.

Sen, A. (2010). The Mobile and the World. *Information Technologies and International Development* 6 (special issue):1–3.

Smith, A., Fressoli, M. and Thomas, H. (2014). Grassroots Innovation Movements: Challenges and Contributions. *Journal of Cleaner Production* 63(0):114–24.

Smith, M.L., Spence, R. and Rashid, A.T. (2010). Mobile Phones and Expanding Human Capabilities. *Information Technologies and International Development* 7(3):77–88.

Talyarkhan, S., Grimshaw, D.J. and Lowe, L. (2005). *Connecting the First Mile: Investigating Best Practice for ICTs and Information Sharing for Development*. Rugby: ITDG.

Thomas, J.J. and Parayil, G. (2008). Bridging the Social and Digital Divides in Andhra Pradesh and Kerala: A Capabilities Approach. *Development and Change* 39(3):409–35.

UNDP. (2012). Mobile Technologies and Empowerment: Enhancing Human Development through Participation and Innovation. In: United Nations Development Programme, New York.

Unwin, T. (2009). *ICT4D: Information Communication Technology Development*. Cambridge: Cambridge University Press.

Van den Hoven, J. (2007). ICT and Value Sensitive Design. In: Goujon, P., Lavelle, S., Duquenoy, P., Kimppa, K. and Laurent, V. (eds), *The Information Society: Innovations, Legitimacy, Ethics and Democracy*. Boston, MA: Springer, pp. 67–72.

Van Reijswoud, V. (2009). Appropriate ICT as a Tool to Increase Effectiveness in ICT4D: Theoretical Considerations and Illustrating Cases. *Electronic Journal on Information Systems in Developing Countries* 38(9):1–18.

Vaughan, D. (2011). The Importance of Capabilities in the Sustainability of Information and Communications Technology Programs: The Case of Remote Indigenous Australian Communities. *Ethics and Information Technology* 13(2):131–50.

Wahid, F. and Furuholt, B. (2012). Understanding the Use of Mobile Phones in the Agricultural Sector in Rural Indonesia: Using the Capability Approach as Lens. *International Journal of Information and Communication Technology* 4(2/3/4):165–78.

Walsham, G. and Sahay, S. (2006). Research on Information Systems in Developing Countries: Current Landscape and Future Prospects. *Information Technology for Development* 12(1):7–24.

Wresch, W. (2007). 500 Million Missing Web Sites: Amartya Sen's Capability Approach and Measures of Technological Deprivation in Developing Countries. In: Rooksby, E. and Weckert, J. (eds), *Information Technology and Social Justice*. Hershey, Information Science Publishing.

Zheng, Y. (2007). Exploring the Value of the Capability Approach for E-development (working paper no. 157). In: *Department of Management, Information Systems Group, London School of Economics and Political Science*. London.

Zheng, Y. (2009). Different Spaces for e-Development: What Can We Learn from the Capability Approach. *Information Technology for Development* 15(2):66–82.

Zheng, Y. and Stahl, B.C. (2012). Evaluating Emerging ICTs: A Critical Capability Approach of Technology. In: Oosterlaken, I. and Van den Hoven, J. (eds), *The Capability Approach, Technology and Design*. Dordrecht: Springer.

Zheng, Y. and Walsham, G. (2008). Inequality of What? Social Exclusion in the e-Society as Capability Deprivation. *Information Technology and People* 21(3):222–43.

CONCLUSION

Technology has played a role in the development of human societies throughout history. When in the 1950s the former colonial powers started to give development aid to countries in the global South, technology became an important focus area. Modernization and technology transfer were seen as essential ingredients of economic development and progress. In the 1970s and 1980s the appropriate technology movement challenged this dominant view on technology and development, which led to many lively debates and a rich pallet of scholarly and practical initiatives (Willoughby 1990). After the 1980s attention for technology in development cooperation diminished, yet has also never been completely absent. Since the 1970s non-governmental organizations focusing on technology 'have been springing up across the developed world' – examples are Engineers without Borders, Engineers for a Sustainable World, Engineering World Health, International Development Enterprises, and KickStart (Riley 2008: 77). Some organizations (like Practical Action, formerly known as the Intermediate Technology Development Group) have been functioning for decades, others (like KickStart) are of a more recent origin. Universities still do work in the area of engineering and design for development (Kandachar et al. 2011; Moskal et al. 2008) – although perhaps not on such a massive scale as during the heyday of the appropriate technology movement. New movements have sprung up which have incorporated some of the ideas from the appropriate technology movement, like 'technology for social inclusion' in Latin America (Smith et al.

2014). New ideas have entered the debate about technology and human development, such as about the role of entrepreneurship (Kandachar and Halme 2008; Polak and Warwick 2013). And new technologies have led to new fields of activity, the most notable one being ICT for Development, or ICT4D (Unwin 2009).

What this book has focused on is the different ways in which the capability approach, being a general conceptual framework, can be brought to bear on debates about technology and its design, and their contribution to human development. The Introduction explained the core concepts and ideas of the capability approach to the reader. This included the distinction between functionings and capabilities, the need to make an ethical evaluation of capabilities, and the value of both well-being and agency. Technology has in this book been understood as a set of material artefacts, or systems consisting of such artefacts, designed to perform certain functions. The introduction gave some examples of the different ways in which technical artefacts relate to valuable individual human capabilities. It proposed that understanding the relation between human capabilities and technical artefacts requires an iterative movement between 'zooming in' on the details of design and 'zooming out' to see the socio-technical embedding of technologies. A core claim made in the introduction was furthermore that the capability approach needs to be supplemented with technology and design accounts, and several examples of potentially useful accounts have been given throughout the book.

Chapter 1 positioned the capability approach versus some broad and general ideas about how technology contributes to poverty reduction. Reference was made to three basic views distinguished by Leach and Scoones (2006): the 'race to the top', the 'race to the universal fix' and 'the slow race' – with the appropriate technology movement being a variety of that last view. It was argued that the capability approach shares an emphasis on human diversity with the appropriate technology movement, which proposed specific design solutions in response to facts of social, economic and environmental diversity (Oosterlaken et al. 2012). On the other hand the capability approach can be said to go beyond the ideas of the appropriate technology movement in some ways (Fernández-Baldor et al. 2012, 2014). The value of agency and the issue of gender were discussed as examples of where the capability approach has added value. The chapter ended with a critical discussion of what is really core to the capability approach, and concluded that as a general conceptual framework it still allows for many different views on how to make technology work for human development. Thus one may very well accept the capability approach as the best overall account of the meaning and ends of development, while rejecting ideas of the appropriate technology movement about the best means to achieve development. Yet it is hoped that the in-depth discussion of the appropriate technology movement from the perspective of the capability approach will have helped the reader to get a better grasp of what the capability approach is about, as well as its benefits and limitations.

Chapter 2 discussed the importance of engineering or product design for the expansion of valuable human capabilities. A distinction was drawn between two related 'design applications' of the capability approach. First, in the 'narrow' usage the capability approach is seen as presenting a proper conceptualization of individual well-being, namely in terms of the capabilities that a person has. The aim of design is then to contribute to the expansion of these capabilities, to which I referred as 'design for capabilities' or 'capability sensitive design' (a variation on the idea of the existing value sensitive design approach). This requires, among others, that designers take relevant conversion factors proactively into account. Next, the two challenges that Van de Poel (2012) has raised for design for well-being more broadly were discussed, namely an epistemological and an aggregation challenge. Second, in a 'broad' usage of the capability approach the value of agency also comes into play. On the one hand agency should be a consideration in design as a process. Participatory design can – depending on its exact implementation – be a way to respect people's agency in the design process. Some have however argued that respect for agency in addition require implementing policies that expand people's capability to do design themselves (Dong 2008). Agency is also a value consideration when judging the outcome of design, as technical artefacts can give people more or less freedom to realize the functionings of their choice. In reality both the narrow and the broad usage of the capability approach in design should go hand in hand.

Chapter 3 argued that individual human capabilities are actually very much dependent on the existence of enabling groups and social structures. This means that an individual's capabilities are relational and contextual. It was then discussed how technical artefacts need to be properly embedded in the surrounding socio-technical networks or structures in order to have the intended effect on individual capabilities. The concept of 'conversion factors', which is so often used in the capability approach, is not always able to capture the complexity of such networks/structures. The second part of the chapter reflected technology and individual freedom. Reference was made to Briggle's (2009) distinction between pluralist views of technology and strong system/network views of technology. Both acknowledge that technology is not fully neutral towards the good life. Yet the former holds that a myriad of technologies and technological usage practices exists side by side, giving users a wide range of choices. This seems to imply that in general technology ought to be promoted, as the availability of more technologies will mean that people will have more capabilities, and in that way are empowered to realize their own view of the good life. According to the latter view, however, many technologies only function within larger socio-technical systems or networks, between which individuals cannot always switch that easily and which may be more or less restrictive. This perspective is more pessimistic about the choices and freedoms that people have. Socio-technical systems/network may also diminish some capabilities while expanding others. In this view more public deliberation about technology is needed.

Chapters 2 and 3 suggest two basic, complementary strategies if for example a development organization aims to effectively expand the human capabilities of marginalized groups with the help of technology. On the one hand one may want to make sure – to the degree possible – that the introduction of a certain technical artefact is accompanied by appropriate changes in the surrounding socio-technical networks. On the other hand one may make the design of a technical artefact appropriate – to the degree possible – for the relevant socio-technical network or usage environment as it exists. When adopting the capability approach as a value-based perspective that can guide the design of technical artefacts ('capability sensitive design' or 'design for capabilities'), this should ideally be based on a thorough understanding of the multiple and complex relations between technical artefacts, human capabilities, and the socio-economical–technical environment in which both humans and artefacts are embedded. What Chapter 3 furthermore made clear is that what one sees through the lens of the capability approach will also depend on which 'filters' or technology accounts one adds to this lens, for example a 'pluralist technology theory' or a 'strong system/network view of technology'.

Chapter 4 returned to a contemporary debate on technology and human development, more specifically on ICT4D. The question was asked whether there is anything special about ICT4D that sets it apart from other technologies. Next the chapter discussed various criticisms that capability scholars have voiced on 'mainstream' ICT4D practice. These included: too much emphasis on ICT provision while ignoring conversion factors; too much focus on its impact on economic growth despite the relevance of ICT for many aspects of well-being; and too little attention for people's own ambitions or agency. Next a case from the appropriate technology movement was presented which illustrated the importance of both 'zooming in' on the details of design and 'zooming out' to see the socio-technical embedding of technologies – namely a case of the introduction of mp3 players and podcasts in a rural area in Zimbabwe. Together with the case of telecentres (Ratan and Bailur 2007) this was then used to reflect on the fact that both in the design and implementation/usage phases tensions may arise between well-being and agency as central values in the development process. The capability approach may be used to conceptualize such tensions, but further normative accounts in combination with empirical analysis will be needed to make concrete ethical judgements about cases in which such a tension arises. The chapter ended by discussing how there are many ways to operationalize the capability approach for application to the evaluation of ICT4D projects.

The capability approach is a 'framework of thought' that cannot be straightforwardly operationalized in one single way (Robeyns 2000). In this book the focus has not been on specific empirical applications of the capability approach to technology, but on the capability approach as a general conceptual framework that helps us to critically rethink technology. The capability approach explicitly and persistently puts central *people* and the lives they are able to live – not technology. It asks what people are, all things considered, able to do and be in their lives. This means, according to Robeyns (2011: §2.2), that we must take 'a comprehensive and holistic approach'. On the input side, this means that we should evaluate institutions, social practices and other capability inputs in combination. A piecemeal analysis of a technology's capability impact is thus to be avoided. On the output side, it requires looking at sets of simultaneously achievable capabilities, since sometimes a technology may expand some capabilities while diminishing others. Such a holistic and comprehensive approach is not easy, and the complexity and vagueness of the capability approach has repeatedly been criticized in the past. However, according to Chiappero Martinetti (2008: 69) 'it is precisely the rich and unrestricted nature of the capability approach that makes it so appealing to many researcher, its usefulness in addressing a plurality of issues within a multiplicity of contexts, its interpretive richness regarding what a good life is, and the attention it focusses on human diversity.' It should be noted at this point that the capability approach has already been applied in different ways (Robeyns 2006), such as the assessment of small-scale development projects (including projects introducing a new technology), theoretical and empirical analyses of policies (this could also involve technology policies or the assessment of new technologies) and critiques on social norms, practices and discourses (one could think here of design practices and the ICT4D discourse). Yet many of the empirical applications so far have been concerned with measuring capabilities, while for advancing justice and development 'prospective applications' should also receive attention (Alkire 2008). With that term Alkire means that we should also investigate how the expansion of human capabilities can successfully be brought about. Again, this is not easy. Many technologies, it was remarked in the Introduction, merely expand instrumentally valuable capabilities. Tracing the complex causal links between instrumental capabilities and those capabilities that are ultimately or intrinsically valuable is a challenge (Alkire 2010), but one that we should not avoid.

One advantage of the capability approach, mentioned in Chapter 1, may be worth highlighting again at the end of this book. And that is that 'by starting from [ultimate] ends, we do not a priori assume that there is only one overridingly important means to that ends (such as income), but rather explicitly ask the question which types of means are important for the fostering and nurturing of a particular capability, or set of capabilities' (Robeyns 2011: §2.3) Amartya Sen (1985, 1984) has accused economists of suffering, all too often, from 'commodity fetishism'. Likewise, if one were to single-mindedly focus on technology as the fix for poverty, one could be said to have fallen prey to 'technology fetishism'. Especially engineers might be said to be vulnerable to this affliction,[1] with their keen interest in 'new' technologies. This being a book about technology, it is perhaps hard to avoid the impression that technology is the answer to poverty. Sometimes it may indeed be an important means to solve development problems, sometimes it may be part of the problem. We should judge technology in terms of what ultimately matters: the ability of each and every person to lead a life (s)he has reasons to value. And when taking action to solve problems of poverty we should never assume that technology is the solution, but always keep an open mind to the different ways in which a problem can be framed and the various causes of the problem – both of which may point towards solutions other than technology as being the most appropriate or effective.

Note

1 See e.g. Riley (2008: ch. 2) on engineering mindsets and stereotypes.

References

Alkire, S. (2008). Using the Capability Approach: Prospective and Evaluative Analyses. In: Comim, F., Qizilbash, M. and Alkire, S. (eds), *The Capability Approach: Concepts, Measures and Applications*. Cambridge: Cambridge University Press.

Alkire, S. (2010). Instrumental Freedoms and Human Capabilities. In: Esquith, S.L. and Gifford, F. (eds), *Capabilities, Power, and Institutions: Toward a More Critical Development Ethics*. University Park, Pennsylvania: Pennsylvania State University Press.

Briggle, A. (2009). Technology, the Good Life, and Liberalism: Some Reflections on Two Principles of Neutrality. In: *16th biennial conference of the Society for Philosophy and Technology (SPT 2009: Converging Technologies, Changing Societies)*. University of Twente, Enschede, the Netherlands.

Chiappero Martinetti, E. (2008). Complexity and Vagueness in the Capability Approach: Strengths or Weaknesses? In: Comim, F., Qizilbash, M. and Alkire, S. (eds), *The Capability Approach: Concepts, Measures and Applications*. Cambridge: Cambridge University Press.

Dong, A. (2008). The Policy of Design: A Capabilities Approach. *Design Issues* 24(4): 76–87.

Fernández-Baldor, Á., Boni, A., Lillo, P. and Hueso, A. (2014). Are technological Projects Reducing Social Inequalities and Improving People's Well-being? A Capability Approach Analysis of Renewable Energybased Electrification Projects in Cajamarca, Peru. *Journal of Human Development and Capabilities* 15(1):13–27.

Fernández-Baldor, Á., Hueso, A. and Boni, A. (2012). From Individuality to Collectivity: The Challenges for Technology-Oriented Development Projects. In Oosterlaken, I. and Van den Hoven, J. (eds), *The Capability Approach, Technology and Design*. Dordrecht: Springer.

Kandachar, P., Diehl, J.C., Parmar, V.S. and Shivarama, C.K. (2011). *Designing with Emerging Markets – Design of Products and Services (2011 Edition)*. Delft University of Technology, Delft.

Kandachar, P. and Halme, M. (2008). Farewell to Pyramids – How Can Business and Technology Help to Eradicate Poverty? In: Kandachar, P. and Halme, M. (eds), *Sustainability Challenges and Solutions at the Base of the Pyramid: Business, Technology and the Poor*. Sheffield, UK: Greenleaf.

Leach, M. and Scoones, I. (2006). *The Slow Race: Making Technology Work for the Poor*. London: Demos.

Moskal, B.M., Skokan, C., Munoz, D. and Gosink, J. (2008). Humanitarian Engineering: Global Impacts and sustainability of a Curricular Effort. *International Journal of Engineering Education* 24(1):162–74.

Oosterlaken, I., Grimshaw, D.J. and Janssen, P. (2012). Marrying the Capability Approach, Appropriate Technology and STS: The Case of Podcasting Devices in Zimbabwe. In: Oosterlaken, I. and Van den Hoven, J. (eds), *The Capability Approach, Technology and Design*. Dordrecht: Springer, pp. 113–33.

Polak, P. and Warwick, M. (2013). *The Business Solution to Poverty; Designing Products and Services for Three Billion New Customers*. San Francisco, CA: Berrett-Koehler.

Ratan, A.L. and Bailur, S. (2007). Welfare, Agency and 'ICT for Development'. In: *ICTD 2007 – Proceedings of the 2nd IEEE/ACM International Conference on Information and Communication Technologies and Development*. IEEE, Bangalore, India.

Riley, D. (2008). *Engineering and Social Justice*. San Rafael, CA: Morgan & Claypool.

Robeyns, I. (2000). An Unworkable Idea or a Promising Alternative? Sen's Capability Approach Re-examined. In: *Center for Economic Studies Discussion paper 00.30*. Leuven.

Robeyns, I. (2006). The Capability Approach in Practice. *Journal of Political Philosophy* 14(3):351–76.

Robeyns, I. (2011). The Capability Approach. In: Zalta, E.N. (ed.), *Stanford Encyclopedia of Philosophy*.

Sen, A. (1984). *Resources, Values and Development*. Oxford: Blackwell.

Sen, A. (1985). *Commodities and Capabilities*. Amsterdam/New York: North-Holland.

Smith, A., Fressoli, M. and Thomas, H. (2014). Grassroots Innovation Movements: Challenges and Contributions. *Journal of Cleaner Production* 63(0):114–24.

Unwin, T. (2009). *ICT4D: Information Communication Technology Development*. Cambridge: Cambridge University Press.

Van de Poel, I. (2012). Can We Design for Well-being? In: Brey, P., Briggle, A. and Spence, E. (eds), *The Good Life in a Technological Age*. Abingdon, UK: Routledge.

Willoughby, K.W. (1990). *Technology Choice: A Critique of the Appropriate Technology Movement*. Boulder, CO/San Francisco, CA: Westview.

INDEX

Page numbers in *italics* indicate figures.

actor-network theory (ANT) 82, 100n
adaptive preferences 5, 67, 120
appropriate technology (AT) movement: aims and influence 23–4; community participation 29–31, 122; gender issues 32–3, 38; general principles 24–6; innovation criticisms 40–1; specific characteristics approach 26–7

Bailur, Savita 119–22
Basalla, George 48
bicycle use: cultural impact 4–5, 8, 16n; culturally led design 51–2, 64; development indicator 1–2; functionings and capabilities 3–4, 7–8, 50–1; socio-technical embedding of artefacts 86–7
Bijker, Wiebe E. 51–2
Bike4Care 8
Bill and Melinda Gates Foundation 21
Briggle, Adam 90–2, 93, 94

capability approach: aims and purpose 2, 3; appropriate technology principles compatibility 22–3, 26; ICT4D research potential 104–6, 126–31; individualistic focus, limitations of 79, 142; individuals and social structures 79–81; interpretation, differences analysed 34–8; operationalization 70–2; technology related research 10–12; types of capabilities *10*
capability innovation 63–4
capability sensitive design *see* design for capabilities
Chilecompra (e-procurement) 128, 130
collective capabilities 9, *10*, 29–31
community participation: power and gender issues 31, 109–10; technology choice, varied access 29–30, 122–6
conversion factors: core concept 3–5; design elements 56–7; gender sensitivity 33–4, 109; human diversity 22, 27–8, 31–2; localised application 61–2, 115–16; socio-technical embedding 86–8, 115–17
critical theory 85–6
Crocker, David A. 5, 29, 37

Delft University of Technology 71–2
Deneulin, Severine 96, 97–8
design for capabilities: aggregation issues 62; epistemological or knowledge challenge 59–62, 89–90; interconnected solutions 57–8, 61–2, 139; universal/inclusive design 56–7; value and goal combination 62–4; value hierarchy 60–1; value sensitive design 60
development perspectives (race analogy): 'race to the top' (economic growth) 20–1; 'race to the universal fix' 21–2; 'slow race' 22–3
Dong, Andy 69–70

external capabilities 105–6

Fernández-Baldor, Álvaro 29–30, 33–4, 38
functionings and capabilities: capability-functioning distinction 96–9; community participation 29–31; core concept 5–8; multiple realization 96–7; participatory design 68–70, 117–18, 124–5; personal determination 5–7, 47–8, 93–4; persuasive or behaviour-steering design 65–8, *68*, 92–3; technical artifacts, role of 49–50, 64–5

gender issues: cultural practices 32–3, 38, 88–9, 109, 115; inequality and capability approach 33–4, 37–8
good life: interpretation differences 47, *48*, 90–2, *92*; technical artifacts, role of 48–9; valuable capabilities 47–8
Grimshaw, David 122–3
Gudza, Lawrence 122–3

Hartmann, Dominik 39–40
human agency: appropriate technology 29–30; functionings and capabilities 5–6, 47–8; ICT access, preferred vs. prescribed 119–26; interpretation differences 36–7; localised application 27–8; participatory design 68–70, 117–18; persuasive or behaviour-steering design 65–8, *68*, 92–3, 101n; technical artifact usage 64–5

ICT for Development (ICT4D): capability approach criticism 104–6, 126–31, 140–1; choice framework, applications 128–9; information, access and usage 109–11, 113–14, 122–3; NGOs and well-being dilemma 119–22, 125–6; participatory evaluation 111–12, 117–18, 124–5; political interference 123–4; theoretical evidence limited 104; well-being, potential contribution 107–9, 113–16
individualism categories 79
innovation economics 9, *10*
intrinsically valuable capabilities 6–7, *10*

Johnstone, Justine 47–8, 49, 50
justice: central value 7, 9; distributive 110, 130; Nussbaum's interpretation 36, 56–7, 73n, 120; social 69–70

KickStart 40–1
Kleine, Dorothea: choice framework 127–9, *129*; determinism continuum concept 124, *125*, 126; ICT and development 105, 107–8, 112, 119; telecentres, value of 108, 109–10
Kullman, Kim 87–8

Lawson, Clive 82–4, 85, 100n
Leach, Melissa 19–23, 39
Lee, Nick 87–8
Local Content Local Voice project 25–6, 32–3, 38, 113–18, *117*, 122–5

methodological individualism 85

Nussbaum, Martha: capability approach advocate 2; combined capabilities 80, 96–7; control of one's environment 69, 88–9, 120; good life defined 47; interpretation differences 35–6; justified promotion of functioning 66, 97–8; valuable capabilities 7, 55, 59, 61; views debated 96

Index **147**

One Laptop per Child (OLPC) programme 87–8

participatory design 68–70, 117–18, 124–5
philosophers of technology 49, 55, 65, 84, 93, 100n
plurist theorists of technology 90–1, 97
poverty reduction and technology: capability approach benefits 21, 22, 40; complementary strategies 39–40; economic growth (race to top) 20–1; global intervention (universal fix) 21–2, 27, 87–8; human diversity and local factors 27–8; localised projects (slow race) 22–3
Practical Action: appropriate technology advocate 24; information sharing through mp3s 25–6, 32–3, 38, 113–18, 122–5; micro power generation 29–30

Ratan, Aishwarya 119–22
Robeyns, Ingrid: capability approach 3, 10, 11, 16n; ethical individualism 79–80; functionings and capabilities 5, 6, 22; gender sensitivity 33, 37; human agency 29; interpretation of approach 35–6, 42n

science and technology studies (STS) 50–1, 85–6, 93
Scoones, Ian 19–23, 39
Sen, Amartya: capability approach advocate 2; 'commodity fetishism' 22; conversion factors 3–5; critic's view 96; good life defined 47; human agency 6, 10, 29, 68, 100n; interpretation differences 35–6; mobile phones and development 103–4; valuable capabilities 7, 29, 59
Seward, Caroline *see* Smith, Matthew L.
Shiva, Vandana 23
Smith, Matthew L. 80–1, 84–5, 99n
social structures: casual mechanisms 80–1; positioned practices 83
socio-technical embedding: capability approach limitations 89–90; combined theories for analysis 85–6; conversion factors 86–8, 115–17;
social practices, impact of 88–9, 98; summarized analysis 94–6, 139–40; technological design 82–4
socio-technical network/systems 91–3, *92*, 97, 98
Stahl, Bernd Carsten 85–6

technical artifacts: capability and social structure interrelationships 82–4, 85, 88–9, 116–18, *117*; connection to good life 48–9; connection to human capabilities 49–50, 52; social practices, impact of 50, *51*, 51–2, 58
technological design: capability-functioning distinction 64–5; capability sensitive 54, 55–8; human-centred, limitations of 54–5; operationalization of capability approach 70–2; persuasion and behaviour-steering 65–8, *68*, 84; social context 59–60; socio-technical embedding 82–4, 140; user participation and policy 69–70; value sensitive 53–4
technology: behaviour-steering 65–8; capability approach limitations 11–12; research scarcity 10–11
technology-capability relationship: instrumental and intrinsic values 7–9, 50–2; 'zooming in-zooming out' perspective 14, *15*, *117*, 117–18
telecentres 108, 109–10, 119

UN Development Programme: technology focus (2001 report) 20, 21, 23, 39
universal/inclusive design 56–7

values, conception interpretation 61
value sensitive design 53–4, 60–1
Van de Poel, Ibo 58–61
Van den Hoven, Jeroen 48–50, 91

well-being: conception, interpretation of 61; conversion factors 56–7; design for capabilities 55–8; human-centred design, limitations of 54–5; ICT, potential contribution

107–9, 113–16; ICT use, preferred vs. prescribed 119–22; multidimensional capabilities 62–4, 84; NGOs and well-being dilemma 125–6; personal determination 3, 6

Willoughby, Kelvin 25, 26, 28

Zheng, Yingqin 85–6, 111–12, 127
Ziegler, Rafael 63–4